FRITZ

Leutnant der Reserve Nagel, 1916

The World War I Memoirs
of a German Lieutenant

by
Fritz Nagel

Edited by
Richard A. Baumgartner

DER ANGRIFF PUBLICATIONS: Huntington, W.Va.

First published in 1981 by
DER ANGRIFF PUBLICATIONS,
1024 Sixth Street,
Huntington, West Virginia   25701
U.S.A.

© 1981 Fritz Nagel

ISBN 0-9604770-0-4

To my loving family.

Fritz Nagel

Contents

FRITZ

FOREWORD

War is a very uncomfortable business. You should avoid it if at all possible.

Fritz Nagel

I first met Fritz Nagel at his Paducah, Ky., home in late March 1980. Beginning with our initial handshake, I was impressed with his spry spirit and only slightly veiled wit that "broke the ice" immediately. During the drive home two days later, I realized my visit was something I would not soon forget.

The youngest son of Rudolf and Wilma Nagel of Bremen, Karl Friedrich Ludolf Nagel was born August 6, 1892. "But nobody ever called me Karl, Friedrich or Ludolf," he laughingly told me when pressed for his full name.

"Fritz" turned 22 years old on August 6, 1914 — the same day he pulled on the feldgrau tunic of the German field artillery for the first time. War in Europe had broken out only days before and, although he had served previously in the army as a one-year volunteer, Nagel, by his own admission, was completely unprepared emotionally for the coming ordeal. The sense of duty propelled him through Belgium and France in the war's early days. But even that was nearly undermined as continuous hunger, lack of sleep and exhaustion gnawed at Nagel's health, sending him home to Germany in late 1914 with dysentery.

Through his father's urging, Nagel wrote down his experiences of the first four months of the war while recuperating in Bremen. This encouraged him to keep a daily diary for the rest of the conflict when he returned to service in January 1915. These now fading inscriptions form the backbone of Nagel's memoirs as a Frontsoldat of the First World War.

In 1962, 50 years after he initially enlisted in the German army, Nagel penned his account of military life, and death, during the years 1912 to 1921. Based for the most part on his war diaries, Nagel's narrative should not be viewed as a work of pretentious scholarship, to be compared with other accounts written by veterans with more literary flair. As he states in his introduction, Nagel originally was induced to begin

1

writing because, "One day maybe my grandchildren would like to read what their grandfather thought and did in those days."

Nonetheless, Nagel's wartime memoirs are laced with candor, honesty, pathos and humor that still typify the man today. From a one-year volunteer in the artillery to a lieutenant in several successful anti-aircraft units by war's end, what Nagel "thought and did in those days" is reflected vividly, but simply, on the following pages.

Militarily, Nagel was credited officially with having shot down two enemy airplanes from the ground, as recorded in **Der Nachrichtenblatt der deutschen Luftstreitkräfte**, which was issued by the Commanding General of the Air Service, Wilhelm von Hoeppner. Anti-aircraft units — a natural outgrowth of the military applications of aviation during the period 1914 to 1918, and which Nagel was associated with for 47 months — became integral parts of most of the major combatants' armies both offensively and defensively.

At first, however, the chances of shooting down an airplane high in the sky with an artillery piece located on terra firma were minute at best. Pure luck brought only periodic success in the war's early days, as Nagel explains. But with technological and theoretical improvements in such things as weapons and rangefinding optics, and better training of officers and men, anti-aircraft — or "Archie," as it was called by many of the war's participants — proved a viable form of waging warfare.

Nagel's principal antagonists during the war were men flying in the wooden, fabric and metal machines displaying the tricolor roundel markings of the Allies. One of these fliers — Capt. William C. Lambert, an American 22-victory ace who served with 24 Squadron RFC/RAF in 1918 — paid tribute to the potential threat that German anti-aircraft fire posed to life in an open cockpit. In his book "Combat Report," Lambert wrote:

"We seemed to be the only airplanes in the sky. Archie was taking some pot-shots at us but none came close. This was my first encounter with anti-aircraft fire and I was scared. You would see a black burst of smoke and hear a loud cough. The first burst might be above you; the second below but much closer. He had your range now and would do better on the third try. The burst you hear will not hurt you — it has already gone by. But watch out for the one you do not hear. You start zig-zagging, slow down or speed up. You change altitude, up or down about 200 feet. If you do not do so that third shot might be "it." You could have a lot of fun with Archie once you were acquainted with him. If you watched carefully you might even locate him and, feeling very brave, go down and attack him. Do not think for one minute that he always missed. He had brought down many of our aircraft."

This episode described by Lambert occurred on April 2, 1918. That same day, German anti-aircraft batteries on the Western Front received credit for shooting or forcing down three Allied planes — two Sopwith Camels and a Spad. And, only six days before, Nagel and his crew had shot down a British two-seater.

But, amid what is essentially a war story, Nagel's narrative cannot hide one other, underlying facet of his account — a genuine love for his late wife, Dorothy.

Dorothy Frances Lane, the daughter of prominent English surgeon Hugh Clifford Lane, met Fritz while he was in Switzerland in 1912, learning to speak better French. As Nagel explained, "I fell in love with Dorothy and naturally wanted to induce her mother to move the family to Bremen. Dorothy had a brother who was two years older. He wanted a job, so I got him one in my father's firm. Her mother had the means to live wherever she wanted to. When the war broke out in 1914 the American consul offered to arrange their moving back to England. But I told them the war would be over in 30 days or so. Why move?"

Thus, as an enemy alien, Dorothy was "forced" to remain in Bremen for the next four years — much more a prisoner of love than of war. Fritz and Dorothy were married in his parents' home during Nagel's transfer from the Eastern Front to France in 1917.

An additional side to Nagel's story can be found in the photograph sections following each chapter. Most of the photos are from Nagel's own albums. From January 1915 on, he wore a small cased camera on his belt in lieu of a revolver, and took pictures whenever an opportunity presented itself.

Sincere appreciation for a wide range of generous assistance in the preparation and publishing of this memoir must be offered to the following people:

William K. Combs, who first brought my attention to Nagel's manuscript and who introduced me to Fritz; and Laurence M. Strayer and Jerry Raisor, whose help and friendship always merit special thanks.

Paul and Leona Smith's painstaking and diligent efforts proved invaluable in ways too numerous to mention. Paul's artistic skills and technical abilities were of paramount importance in the production and completion of the book.

Fellow Society of World War I Aero Historians members Peter Kilduff and Frank W. Bailey lent their expertise in times of need and supplied ample amounts of encouragement.

Finally, a special note of appreciation must be extended to Fritz Nagel himself, for without his story, this book would not exist.

Richard A. Baumgartner
Huntington, West Virginia — June 1980

Mr. Baumgartner, a native of Menomonee Falls, Wisconsin, and a journalism graduate of the University of Missouri, is graphics editor of the Herald-Dispatch in Huntington, West Virginia. His interest in World War I history spans 13 years, with the past several years devoted to accumulating personal accounts of German veterans of all branches of the Imperial German army.

INTRODUCTION

I have written these World War I memoirs without being very clear in my own mind why I was doing it. My adventures were not unusual, but history moves so very fast. Friends of today are the enemies of tomorrow. Wars come and go and people soon forget. How many Americans today can tell who were Germany's allies and therefore America's enemies in that conflict?

The youth of today knows but little about the events and causes of that long and bloody war. For the United States it was a short war. When it entered and appeared on the battlefield for the first time, the worst fighting was over. The war did not last long enough to create many American heroes and American literature about it is limited. Perhaps one day my grandchildren would like to read what their grandfather thought and did in those days, now almost forgotten.

The war lasted from August 4, 1914, to November 11, 1918, and to me, these were an awfully long four years and three months. Germany and its allies — Austria-Hungary, Turkey and Bulgaria, tried in vain to beat the combined armies and navies of France, England, Canada, Australia, New Zealand, Russia, Italy, Belgium, Serbia, Romania and the United States.

The fact the most powerful nations were aligned against us made me feel from the beginning that our diplomats must be incompetent, or there must be something in the German way of doing things offensive to our neighbors. I could not understand it.

During the war I kept a daily diary and it is now easy for me to find out what I did and what happened on any certain date. I remember the events but cannot connect faces with the many names appearing on the pages of my diary. Now, so many years later, the events seem so impersonal, as if they happened to somebody else. It seems difficult to connect my present self to the happenings of so many years ago.

Writing about that war I must be careful not to look at it through the spectacles of a man that much older. I was 22 years old when it started. Until then, life had been comfortable and easy. Emotionally I was completely unprepared for the coming ordeal. Technically I had the advantage of one year's training in the army, but that I might be forced to really fight one day never entered my mind. To be trained as a soldier was a normal way of life for every healthy German boy, but to me it seemed more like playing soldiers than actual training for combat.

When war broke out I was crushed. It all seemed like a bad dream and could not be true. My plans to go to the United States as a tobacco buyer for my father's tobacco import firm and join my brother already in Paducah, Ky., now seemed as far away as a trip to the moon.

On August 4, 1914, I had to put on the fieldgray war uniform of the German field artillery for the first time. I was a private first class and felt caught in a huge trap. I disliked any kind of military life because it was full of discomforts and so contrary to my nature. My military ambitions were zero. I could not understand at all why all the soldiers now marching to the troop trains were apparently so happily singing and shouting. We had not won the war yet. To my mind there was nothing to be so happy about. It was quite impossible for me to join in the general enthusiasm.

It has always been my belief that no nation wanted this war, but at that time, there was no machinery to prevent it. International diplomacy was conducted secretly and the final decisions leading to peace or war were concentrated in just a few hands. The general public or its representatives had nothing to do with it. England and France were democracies. Germany, Austria-Hungary, Italy, Russia, Serbia, Romania and Bulgaria were autocratic one-man monarchies. One of the main drawbacks to a last-minute peaceful solution was the entanglements of the various alliances.

When the rather unknown Austrian archduke was shot and killed by a Serbian student during an inspection trip in newly occupied territory (the ownership of which had been a matter of dispute between Austria and Serbia for many years), a chain reaction took place which simply could not be stopped. Austria demanded punishment of the murderer and an apology from the Serbian government. Serbia promised punishment but refused to apologize. Germany urged its ally, Austria-Hungary, not to push the matter towards armed conflict. At this time, the Austro-Hungarian empire was beginning to crack up. But to its leaders, it seemed a good opportunity to show the world that it was still a powerful nation, which, as everyone knew in case of war, would be backed up by Germany. Austria sent Serbia an ultimatum. Russia mobilized, declaring it would resist an invasion of Serbia. Now Germany became frightened and mobilized. Since 1909, France had entered a military pact with Russia as mutual protection against Germany. Frantic last-minute cables were exchanged between the Kaiser and the Czar. All to no avail — matters were now in the hands of the generals, and the only solution they knew was to fight. Fight quickly and with all your might. The German general staff knew that only a quick victory could save Germany from defeat.

The only country not involved in these various military pacts was England. But an invasion of Belgium, whose neutrality England had guaranteed, would bring England in immediately on the side of our enemies.

The lights over Europe went out. Now it was a question of bare survival. The house was on fire; let's all try to put it out as soon as possible. It's better to kill than to be killed, although I hoped I would never see an enemy, towards whom I had no bad feelings whatever. Great villians like Hitler did not appear on the international scene. The German soldier saw no reason to hate anybody. During my time in the army I never heard an officer or soldier even discuss our enemies in personal terms. On the other side, men were forced by circumstances to fight for their countries, just as we were. It was a calamity engulfing all civilized mankind. We did not know whom to blame.

Fritz Nagel
Paducah, Kentucky — Summer 1962

ONE

1912-1913

A one-year volunteer

My military career started in October 1912. All healthy Germans had to serve in the army. After an easy examination, those who had attended schools preparing them for higher education could enter any regiment of their choice as so-called "one-year volunteers." After one year's service, they had the right to further training to eventually become reserve officers — all in all, a process of several years off-and-on training. The greatest proportion of the soldiers (93 per cent) did not have the required higher education and had to serve two years in the infantry or artillery, or three years in the horse artillery or cavalry. They had no choice and no chance for promotion unless they wished to enlist in the regular army after their two or three years of service, in which case, the highest rank obtainable was sergeant.

I chose the Hessian Field Artillery Regiment Nr. 11 because a friend of the family had served in the regiment and liked it. The bulk of the regiment was stationed in Kassel, but the two batteries of its horse artillery (the crews rode on horses instead of sitting on the guns) were stationed in Fritzlar, near Kassel, a very small town of 3,500 people, founded about 800 A.D. For soldiers it offered no attractions whatever. Narrow cobbled streets, one restaurant, no movies.

As potential officer candidates, we were supposed to live like gentlemen. This type of one year's service in a good regiment of the artillery or cavalry was expensive and only parents with means could afford to send their sons. Boys who had the required schooling and social background, but not the money, could serve with the infantry and choose a regiment stationed in their hometown.

From the first day on I had to have a batman to take care of my uniforms and another batman to take care of my horse, which was my own and for which I had to pay for the fodder, etc. I had to pay for all uniforms and several were required, from dress to work denim. And things like dress swords and white leather gloves cost money! We were supposed to eat in the officers' mess and live in our own flats or rooms. This one year cost my father 7,500 marks, or about $1,800, a large sum in those days, considering a soldier received eight cents a day or $29 a year. In civilian life the sum of 7,500 marks would have enabled anyone to live very comfortably in a nice house, have a servant and feed the family well.

Our regiment was a very old one. It was first mentioned in Hessian history in 1427 and from then on it fought in all wars in which the archduke of Hesse was involved. In 1776 the regiment was sold or loaned to Great Britain to fight in the American Revolution. King George III paid each soldier 117 marks and the officers considerably more. Great Britain also guaranteed to replace all materiel lost in the colonies. On April 14, 1776, the British picked up a total of 7,400 Hessians — infantry, artillery and cavalry — in Bremen. They landed on Staten Island 98 days later, more dead than alive. Heavy storms almost foundered the whole expedition. The regiment later participated in battles around Long Island, White Plains, Trenton and Germantown. There is still a written report in the regimental archives from a certain Captain Krug, who reported under the date of October 1, 1777, that he fired on General Washington and his staff whom he recognized "across the river."

After the Revolutionary War many of these Hessian soldiers settled in the then 13 states. Quite a number already had deserted. General Washington promised a deserter 50 acres of land. A captain coming over to the American side would receive 800 acres, four oxen, one bull, two cows and four pigs. Or they could settle in Canada where an officer, according to rank, could obtain 1,500 to 3,000 free acres, plus enough cash to establish himself.

I knew that my chances for promotion in the regiment were practically zero. Only those one-year men willing to go on with training after their year's service would be chosen as officer candidates. Young men from families engaged in overseas import or export usually went abroad and in case of war, would be lost to the army. Other one-year men never would be promoted to officer rank because they did not meet the required social standing. Nothing was written about it and each regimental commander had his own standards. But in our regiment, no son of a family which earned its living by working with its hands would be promoted to officer rank. That included all store owners, all service trades, all peasants and all Jews.

The purpose was to create an officer elite, not connected by blood or friendship with the common soldiers they had to command in case of war. The standards were relaxed during the war, but not much. Promotion of enlisted men or non-commissioned officers to officer rank on the battlefield was unknown in the German Army.

A certain amount of glamor was supposed to surround every German boy serving in a good regiment. I could not find fun or glamor anywhere. I found nothing at all to compensate for the many discomforts connected with training.

Service started at 4 a.m. and ended at 6 p.m., with a half hour for midday lunch. This consisted of a sandwich quickly wolfed down. Riding lessons and drilling took place hour after hour every day, rain or shine, except Sundays. Instant reaction to a given situation and blind obedience were the goals. We had to make stiff and formal salutes to every superior we met, from corporal to colonel. We saluted hundreds of times each day. After a few weeks of that I felt more like a machine than a human being. And nobody spoke to us. In our battery we were five one-year men completely separated socially from the others. We were still considered common soldiers.

But I liked the riding aspect of the service. We had really fine horses and the maneuvers with the cavalry were glittering affairs. To see several regiments of lancers, hussars and dragoons, all in their rather gaudy peacetime uniforms, mount an attack at full speed was a thrilling spectacle. Lances down, they thundered across a large field. One stumbling horse could topple half a regiment.

The high command evidently still believed in the effectiveness of massed cavalry attacks. Cavalry had played a big part in the American Civil War as well as in the Franco-German war of 1870, but it already was felt that even massed cavalry did not carry enough punch, except against an enemy on the verge of collapse. For that reason two riding batteries were added to each cavalry division. We had the same firepower and the same equipment as the 7.7 centimeter field artillery, but could move much faster. Our guns could be pulled at full gallop across a ditch — a gun might jump into the air and almost topple over but we carried no crew sitting on the guns. Everybody was mounted and speed was of the essence. An attack might be ordered for the cavalry. It was then our job to soften up the enemy and do it fast.

Our horses were beautiful animals, specially bred and all of one color — black in our battery. They had enough Arabian blood to be spirited but not too much of it. As for speed we were quite able to keep up with the cavalry.

These maneuvers were held on large military training reservations and were extremely strenuous. Men and horses constantly were bathed in perspiration as the exercises went on hour after hour. It soon became clear to me that a captain commanding a riding battery had no easy job. He commanded six guns, each drawn by six horses, plus all the officers, NCOs and crew, a total of some 92 mounted men who looked to the captain in front for the next command galloping at full speed. Command by voice could not be heard and the battery was commanded by arm signal. The captain had to know whether his battery could negotiate the field in front of it. An unseen hedge or fence could be fatal; he had to know exactly when to give the stop signal so the battery was in the best position for effective firing. To suddenly stop a mass of fast running horses pulling guns took horsemanship acquired only by endless training. A frontal forward move, even at high speed, was a relatively simple exercise, but to have the battery move at full speed around the wing gun and still wind up with all the guns in one line wheel to wheel, 15 yards apart, was difficult. Correct timing was the key to success. Once the horses were brought to a stop, we would jump off cowboy fashion, unhook the gun from the ammunition wagon and have it ready for firing in less than a minute.

It was plenty of exercise and our heavy uniforms did not make things easier. Our riding breeches were of heavy wool lined with leather down the legs and on the seat. The blue coat with brass buttons, high black stiff collar and broad white leather belt made it difficult when endlessly jumping on or off the horses. And our ornate and hot helmet could only be kept from falling off by keeping the chin strap very tight.

A single machine-gun or one or two shrapnel shells exploding at the right places could quickly create chaos in a real war. Horsedrawn artillery was very vulnerable to enemy action, I thought. I could not see how such a clumsy outfit could survive for long. Neither could I understand why the cavalry regiments went through mock mass cavalry charges every day. It was a stirring sight seeing thousands of men and horses thundering over a field, but what could they do against enemy artillery or machine-guns? A few infantrymen with well-aimed fire could make horses and men topple over each other.

These cavalry regiments were commanded exclusively by a type of officer now practically extinct. The regimental commanders were dukes, princes and other members of the high-ranking aristocracy. Their fathers and grandfathers had served their kings for many generations and army life was all they knew and cared about. Their family names appeared again and again in every war.

The officers, including the one-year men, would take their meals at night in a huge dining hall. It was the most elegant room I have ever seen. Huge chandeliers were everywhere and the walls were covered with historic paintings of old battles. More than a thousand officers would sit at long, large tables in their dress uniforms of all colors. The atmosphere was gay but restrained. Plenty of wine and champagne was flowing, but nobody would dare drink too much and manners were extremely polite. There was no doubt in my mind that these fellows were the cream of the army. But compared to the richness of the cavalry uniforms, those of us in the artillery looked somewhat like poor relatives.

After these exercises were over we were shipped back to our garrison town of Fritzlar, where our training continued. For one hour every day the one-year men would have lessons in army composition, map reading and tactics, while the duties of an officer in peace and war were explained in detail.

There was no social contact whatever with the civilian population. The soldiers were kept more or less locked up in their barracks and none of the officers or one-year men showed interest in the local girls. For any one of us to be seen with the local plumber's daughter would have meant the end of our military aspirations. However, it must be said that these unwritten regulations concerning the company we were permitted to keep were not quite as unreasonable as they might seem to somebody born and reared in the United States. The girls belonging to the local tradesmen, small farmers and functionaires never had a chance to acquire an education or a taste for a higher standard of living. In those days, class lines were strictly drawn.

Disciplinary problems were very rare. Drunkenness, fighting or being absent without permission were practically unknown. The draftees in our outfit were quiet, orderly and accepted army routine without trouble. All of them were 19 or 20 years old and free of police records. They made fine soldiers.

In September of 1913 we were shipped out of Fritzlar again to a camp for shooting with live ammunition. The battery now had to show what it could do under simulated war conditions.

For two weeks the battery left the barracks at dawn, exercising and shooting for the next 10 hours. By this time the crews were well trained in the manipulation of the guns and worked together smoothly as a team. These shooting exercises evidently were much more a test of the officers than of the crews. In my opinion it was not easy to be a good battery commander. The mistakes or misjudgments he could make were endless. After each shooting the bugler would call all officers to the critique which often took more than an hour and was held out of earshot by the colonel commanding the regiment. We one-year men were not permitted to attend these fault-finding sessions. Our confidence in our officers might be undermined.

These field problems were difficult and required instant decisions. Stationary or moving mechanical targets popped up everywhere and nobody knew when. Movable targets were on rails, criss-crossing the landscape. At that time we had no rangefinders and the commander had to have a good eye for distances. The battery fired from cover if at all possible, and the terrain had to permit the ammo wagons to come in close. The commander had to act fast and give the right commands, otherwise complete confusion would result. Once the battery was in firing position, the commands as to distance, side or wind correction, or whether to shoot shrapnel or shell, had to be given immediately.

The targets were quickly bracketed and blanketed with heavy and very accurate fire. One of the main difficulties always seemed to be a short and accurate description of the target by the commander. Directions like "the target east of the hill" were not acceptable because a soldier might not know where east was in enemy territory. Target description had to be related to plainly visible landmarks, but when there were no special landmarks, it was not so easy to direct all eyes of the battery in the right direction quickly.

On October 1, 1913, I was dismissed as a private first class and my one-year army service was over.

During the war, I met my old battery only once — in Russia. Recognizing the number 11 on the mens' shoulder straps, I quickly saw that it was my old outfit. Some of the NCOs remembered me very well, but the few officers I saw were strangers to me. The battery was on its way for regrouping and rest. A few days before, the German army corps it belonged to, together with two cavalry divisions, had a large number of Russians caught in a pocket. One cavalry division, supported by this battery, was ordered to block the only escape route. They told me it was an impossible task — their six guns and the dismounted cavalry could not hold the Russians. Among the killed in this fight was my old one-year roommate. He was a very fine musician and had sold me one of his violins. I also asked to see my horse again. It had the curious name "Ukraine" and I had no trouble finding it hale and hearty.

Fresh recruits of the 2nd Battery, 11th Hessian Field Artillery Regiment at Fritzlar, October 1912. Nagel stands in the second row, fifth from right.

Nagel, a one-year volunteer in 1913.

Artillery observation platform and command post, summer maneuvers 1913.

Unloading artillery caissons from railroad flatcars, summer maneuvers 1913.

Nagel, summer maneuvers 1913.

TWO

1914

The lights go out

During the last days of July 1914 I was in Antwerp visiting customers of my father's firm while waiting for the North German Lloyd steamer "Berlin," which was supposed to sail for New York on August 3. The newspapers were full of alarming reports, but Germany had not yet ordered full mobilization. My passport said I had to report to the nearest regiment of field artillery on the second day of mobilization.

Our customers were not in the mood to talk business. When I spoke with Belgium's largest dealer in his Antwerp office, he was terribly pessimistic. My thought was that he had nothing to fear for his country because all nations, including Germany, had guaranteed the neutrality of Belgium. He brushed that aside as plain poppycock. France and Germany both knew that they could not defeat each other without outflanking the other through Belgium. That's why everybody was so anxious to prevent the other side from crossing Belgium's borders, or so he claimed. At that moment business was quite impossible as most Belgian businessmen feared the worst. All of this was bad because Bremen warehouses were filled with tobacco from Kentucky, Tennessee, Brazil, Java and Sumatra and had to be sold. Bremen was then the largest tobacco market in the world.

The SS Berlin was to sail in a few days if no mobilization was ordered. The North German Lloyd office in Antwerp could give no worthwhile information. But even if she did sail, despite mobilization, would I get to America? Surely the British navy would stop a German passenger liner in the English Channel and my passport clearly would give me away as a reservist. I did not know what to do. When I reached my hotel I found a telegram from my father urging me to come home quickly.

As I left the hotel, soldiers were suddenly everywhere. I had my small handbag with me but realized that all normal travel seemed impossible and I decided to leave my steamer trunk in storage at the depot. Nobody could tell me whether trains still were running. I thought it best to go to the railroad station and find out for myself.

Hundreds of people were milling around and all kinds of rumors were flying thick and fast: German troops were massing on the Belgian border; England again had guaranteed Belgian neutrality; Russia already was on a full war footing, etc. Inside the depot all kinds of announcements were made and one of them said that all German citizens must report immediately to the official in the passenger waiting room. They would see in my passport that I was a soldier and I feared arrest if German troops really had violated their border. I moved as far away from that waiting room as possible when I saw a train marked "Maastricht" on the platform. It was a town in Holland. As far as I knew no trouble with Holland was brewing so I boarded the train and felt very happy when it pulled away. The train was jammed and with hundreds of others I had to stand up. It was too crammed full for even the conductor to get through and collect tickets. I was lucky because I had none. We reached the Dutch border without trouble and while crossing it I jumped train at a point closest to the German border. I was happy to have escaped safely from Belgium, but I had lost my steamer trunk with all my clothes and camera. I had no idea then that I would be able to claim my trunk in routine fashion when I entered Antwerp as a soldier in April 1916. I presented my claim ticket and the Belgian railroad official had no trouble finding it promptly. Nothing was missing except my camera. The trunk had been opened forcibly and tied back with ropes. Whether the Belgians or Germans had opened it I never found out.

No trains in Holland were running and I had to walk for a few hours before reaching the Dutch-German border.

According to the rules, I would have to present myself to the first field artillery regiment I could find, but that idea disturbed me very much. I would have to go to war with strangers and I could not see my family. I was determined to break this rule and reach Bremen before entering the army. It seemed to me that nobody would be interested enough to find out what had happened to me during these last few hectic days as long as I presented myself as a soldier somewhere.

When I reached Bremen on August 3, my family was frantic. They thought the Belgians had arrested and shot me. The newspapers said so. From then on this sort of wild war propaganda never let up for more than four long years.

August 3 was officially the first day of mobilization. As a reservist I had to present myself to the army on the second day, August 4. War now was certain and people began thinking of what might be ahead. On the streets reservists could be seen everywhere. It seemed as if people were enthusiastic and ready to fight the world at the drop of a hat. I wondered whether this outward show of martial spirit was like whistling in the dark or whether it was genuine. Nobody really could imagine what a real war would bring us.

The German people had the utmost confidence in their army, bordering on adulation. Now everything depended upon our armed forces.

Germany was completely encircled. How could we prevent hordes of enemies from overrunning Germany? But why, and so suddenly, was the whole world determined to destroy us?

The main trouble was the fact the German people had no control whatever over foreign policy and therefore over life and death. Germany was a one-man autocratic empire. The important ministers, such as for foreign affairs, defense, army and navy, were appointed by Kaiser Wilhelm II and unless they carried out his wishes they would be dismissed promptly. The German people elected representatives to the Reichstag in Berlin, but it seemed to me the Reichstag only had a voice in routine matters of no great importance. To criticize this set-up was considered unpatriotic. In fact, the German people were only mildly interested in democracy as such. Why worry? Everything was fine. Germany was prosperous, nobody was mistreated and our progress was faster than in any other country in the world. Only the small leftist groups were clamoring for more representation at the top. But these were the people born on the wrong side of the track — the common workers and the communists. They had no influence.

For all practical purposes, the fate of the nation was in the very few hands of men around the Kaiser. Were they capable? Nobody knew. International diplomacy was conducted in secrecy. No doubt they were honorable men in the ordinary sense of the word. Scandals of one sort or another were unknown. It all boiled down to one question: What kind of a man was the Kaiser?

Although there was no real censorship in Germany, all newspapers were absolutely loyal to the monarchy. To insult the Kaiser was an offense punishable with a prison term. The result of all this was a sort of demi-god attitude toward the man who controlled our destiny. He kept himself quite apart from the people. Only a few ever talked to him. When he came to Bremen all schools were closed and the streets were lined with people. All they saw was a glimpse of him dashing by in a horse-drawn carriage, always wearing an army or navy uniform. I don't believe he owned a civilian's suit of clothes. About his real character, abilty, likes and dislikes, we knew nothing at all.

After the war the German people had a chance to form their own judgments about their ruler for the first time.

———————

Following the 1871 victory over France, the German Chancellor Bismarck forced her to pay the enormous sum of 5 billion francs in gold. Suddenly, the newly united Germany had a huge surplus of money which was well used to build up industry and commerce. The trademark "Made in Germany" became a great success. By 1914, Germany was prosperous.

Trade with the United States was booming and international relations could not have been more friendly. No rivalry or competition existed. Germany bought huge amounts of American raw materials such as cotton and tobacco, and exported industrial machinery and chemicals to America. As a boy I often saw American business friends of my father as house guests. My mother always decorated the dinner table with an American and German flag. That these friendly Americans would ever fight us seemed quite an unimaginable possibility.

Now that war had broken out I gave some thought to the purely military chances. Books about international events, foreign armies and colonial and other wars had always interested me. I tried to reason out what might happen soon.

In Germany every healthy man had to serve in the army, whether laborer or scientist. Nobody was exempt. Modern weapons will make any war a short one and we needed every good man in the front lines. With everybody fighting and nobody working, how long could a war last? It would be the same in France but not in England, where service in the army remained on a voluntary basis until 1916. Russia was an agricultural country and probably could last a long time.

The French army was rated very high. Since its defeat in 1871, it had been reorganized and no doubt would fight with traditional French valor. During the Franco-German war, the French soldier fought with great courage and tenacity and their armies were defeated only because of inferior French generalship. The generals of Napoleon III could not compare with those fighting under Napoleon I. If properly led, the French will always make fine soldiers.

We considered the English army second class because it was so very small and trained primarily for colonial wars or upheavals. Its generals were used to commanding small units and had no experience in commanding armies. All British common soldiers were professionals, consisting mostly of men unable to make a living in any other profession. We considered the English officers undertrained playboys good at such things as polo. The small British Expeditionary Force would only play a small role in the coming battle. Their colonial army, mostly stationed in India, would arrive too late. By that time the war would be over.

We were afraid of the Russians on account of their enormous numbers — more than six million fighting men. During the Russo-Japanese war of 1904-1905, the Russian soldier had shown incredible endurance. Men shot through the chest were known to have walked 10 miles to the next hospital. But their officers were considered quite inferior. The Russian high command showed itself incompetent while fighting the Japanese, who, at that time, had only a second class army by European standards. German military observers reported incredible bungling on the Russian side.

As to our own and only worthwhile ally, Austria-Hungary, German experts were not optimistic. Austrians or Hungarians just never made good soldiers. They liked the good life, good music, good eating and drinking, and it did not seem possible for them to stand up to the Russians for a long time. They would be overwhelmed. On paper the over-all military situation looked gloomy. But perhaps the German army could produce miracles.

Off to war

On August 4, 1914, I presented myself to the army as a reservist and was told I now belonged to the Reserve Field Artillery Regiment Nr. 18, which was forming in Bahrenfeld near Hamburg, about 75 miles northeast of Bremen. Relatives were not allowed near the building where we had to assemble. As soon as I could I gave a message to a little boy so my family knew I would be shipped out to Bahrenfeld within the hour. Relatives were not allowed on the railroad platform either, only Red Cross people who gave us free cigars, cigarettes and candy.

On the troop train I was glad to see friends I knew well from my rowing and tennis clubs. Our families knew each other and that would facilitate the spreading of information as to our whereabouts.

On August 6 I was issued my field gray uniform which I had never worn before. The color was gray-green with dull buttons, the helmet was covered with a gray cloth so the ornaments would not glitter in the sun and the high riding boots were brown and very heavy. The whole outfit was heavy and ill-fitting.

All soldiers and most of the officers were reservists, but the commander, a first lieutenant soon to become a captain, was a regular army officer about 35 to 40 years old. Most of the non-coms were professionals. The horses were reservists, too. Owners of horses — sportsmen, businessmen or farmers — had to register them regularly and the army knew at all times where the horses were. Even in peacetime the owners knew where they had to surrender their horses. Though untrained, the animals had been inspected regularly by army veterinarians and were first-class material.

In a few days serious training and the breaking-in of our battery started. It quickly became evident that the training of us one-year men had been quite insufficient and we soon became a pain in the neck to our top sergeant. It is true that we were neither fish nor flesh. The big farm boys who already had served two or three years in the horse artillery could saddle a horse and harness it to the gun in no time at all. They were trained to feed, water and keep them clean even at night under bivouac conditions in the field. They liked it and did it very well. I had saddled my horse during my one year's training only a dozen times and knew nothing about the little tricks of feeding and watering. As a result I was clumsy and slow. To handle one or two of these unbroken horses all day and night long and have everything ready to go, say at 4 a.m., was more than we one-year men could handle. During our service some soldier was ordered to do all of our heavy work while we were supposed to learn how to be efficient officers. But nobody trusted us yet with a command. This went on for some time. The top sergeant cussed and fussed with me, calling me a shirker and what have you. I made a big mistake by reminding him that I was not trained to do a common soldier's work. This kind of resistance on my part enraged him and he swore to make a good soldier out of me whatever the cost. From that moment on he really gave me hell. I had to do more disagreeable work than anybody else, such as going on guard duty after a long, hard day. The other one-year men had been smart enough not to say anything, although they, too, were just about breaking down under the heavy physical work.

For instance, I did not have strength enough to pull the straps holding the saddle tight and the horses would blow themselves up in a sort of passive resistance. A regular soldier would give the horse a tremendous kick in the belly to let the air out. My kicks were so feeble they made no impression on my horse at all. Soon I was utterly exhausted and wondered how long I could survive under these conditions. I felt I could not last long with that sergeant breathing down my neck day and night. But I had to endure him until one fine day in Belgium he had what would now be called "shell shock." He was sent home and I accidentally heard the battery commander say how happy he was to get rid of that man.

On August 9 we were shipped north to the Danish border for further training. A British or Russian landing was feared from the Baltic Sea and the whole 9th Army Reserve Corps was sent there. This very pretty peninsula called Schleswig-Holstein is only about 90 miles north of Bremen. It has some of the best German farmland. The population was very friendly although we could not help damaging some of the inhabitants' fields. Fine farms with tidy little houses could be seen everywhere. I was quartered in a house near Taarstedt.

The German offensive against France and Belgium had begun and seemed to be a huge success. The enemy was beaten and retreating everywhere. The situation on the Eastern Front, however, was critical. Enormous numbers of Russians were massed on the Prussian border. Would the army be able to protect our borders? All Germany was quivering with apprehension and excitement. All war news came exclusively from the German General Staff as no reporters were allowed in the front lines.

While training in Schleswig-Holstein some defects became quite apparent. How would we be fed? We were hungry all the time. Only the infantry was fed from a soup kitchen on wheels, which followed the troops wherever they went. We were issued bread and meat but had to do the cooking ourselves, each gun crew for itself. Our crew had found a pot somewhere and whenever the battery rested for eating we were given enough time for the water to boil. All we could do was throw the meat in the boiling pot and wonder what would happen next. The food, of course, was terrible. Finding some wood and then digging a little hole to make a fireplace took time. How could we do all this under real war conditions? We soon found out that the army had made no worthwhile preparations to feed an artilleryman in wartime. We were supposed to live more or less off the enemy's land. But that takes some training, too, and was quite difficult to do for a battery moving about from place to place. My eating equipment consisted of one big soup spoon which I wore jammed in the top of my right riding boot. Our tin drinking cup was a bad piece of equipment. Hot coffee would make it impossible to hold in the hand. It should have been equipped with a wooden handle. One of the gun crews had a man who had been a German cook on a Cunard passenger liner. He did his best to teach us, but soon the officers got hold of him.

Entering Belgium

On August 22 the regiment entrained for Belgium together with the rest of our corps. It took us all night to load the six guns, the ammo wagons and other vehicles on flatcars. The men travelled with the horses in closed cars and I found that quite comfortable. It was rumored the train would travel via Kirchweyhe, a village close to Bremen. I wired my family and when we got to the village my parents and my fiancee, Dorothy, were there waiting. For more comfort my head had been shaved, and with dirt ingrained on my hands, the sight of me seemed to depress my family. In an hour or so the train started towards Belgium. Soon the real war would start for us.

The weather was very hot. At least it felt so in our thick uniforms. We reached Aachen on August 25 and crossed the Belgian border shortly thereafter, reaching Liege the same afternoon. Here we saw the first sign of war — some burned-out houses. The enemy was reported near Tirlemont and soon we were ordered to unload and get ready. It took us three hours and finally, late that afternoon, the battery was ready to go and fight. Nobody told us where exactly the enemy was. Were they Belgians, British or French? Nobody knew.

Warfare in Belgium soon became a hideous experience because the population took part in the fight. Whenever they had the chance they shot down German soldiers. Rumors already had spread that the staff of our division, while standing in a marketplace, had been killed by partisan fire coming from a church belfry. There was little defense against that sort of warfare because the streets were full of civilians and so were the houses. Unless they shot first, nobody knew where the enemy was. It was nerve-wracking in the extreme and resulted in savage and merciless slaughter at the slightest provocation. As we marched towards Louvain, most houses of the villages were burning and dead soldiers and civilians lay everywhere. Some were burned black, their arms and legs sticking out stiff as boards. Frightened civilians lined the streets, hands held high as a sign of surrender. Bedsheets hung out of windows for the same purpose. To see those frightened men, women and children was a really terrible sight. By now the German soldier was frightened, too, expecting to be shot at from all sides. I don't know whether these Belgians were ordered to resist or whether it was spontaneous, but it surely served no useful purpose. They could not kill enough Germans to influence events, though it was easy for them to shoot a German and then disappear in a crowd. The marching troops, the crackling of burning houses and the shouted orders made it impossible to hear even the crack of a single shot.

Early the morning of August 27 we were close to the small town of Tirlemont and I wondered why we were not moving. It seemed our battery was all alone and we were marching without infantry cover. A few determined enemy infantrymen could shoot up a battery easily, creating confusion and losses which would have taken hours to repair. The battery commander refused to move on under these circumstances.

It had become known that I was the only one able to speak French fluently. The commander wanted me to ride forward with him on the road to Louvain and find out what was going on. Where was our infantry? I was supposed to speak to the Belgians and gather all possible information.

First we had to ride through Tirlemont which was burning furiously. The heat was terrific and we had to shield our faces with our arms. In front of us was a sea of flames and I wondered how we would ever get through. The inhabitants were milling and running around, trying to save their houses. Some dead were lying in the streets. It seemed we were the only German soldiers among all those Belgians. The lieutenant had his pistol cocked in his left hand and ordered me to do the same to cover our right side. With my left hand I had to hold the reins, with my right hand the pistol, so there was nothing left to cover my face against the tremendous heat. At times I thought my uniform would catch fire. A few minutes later we saw a German army car speed towards us out of the smoke. Its occupants shouted that we must turn back. "You can't get through with your battery. The civilians are firing from every window." It was the first automobile I had seen carrying a steel contraption from front to rear bumper that cut wires strung across the streets meant to decapitate passengers of staff cars. A few officers had had their heads torn off.

We rode back to our battery. The next day we were ordered to proceed through Tirlemont to Louvain, a march of some 15 miles. The situation in Tirlemont had been cleared up and we managed to get through without trouble. Louvain is a very old university town, founded before 1190, with many small and crooked streets. About 45,000 people lived there. To me it seemed as if all of Louvain was afire and I wondered how we could get through the narrow streets with houses burning on both sides. I didn't know what had happened that morning or why the town was burning, but the fate of Louvain with its famous library was very effectively used in enemy propaganda. Today there is a plaque on the door of the library saying, "Destroyed by German fury, rebuilt by American generosity."

The battery marched through Louvain when news was received that soon we would get into battle. The enemy had been located and our division would attack. But nobody knew anything for sure.

It had been three days and nights since we crossed the Belgian border and quick cat naps were all the rest we had, sometimes standing or leaning against a horse. Nobody had taken his clothes off. We were gray with fatigue and too tired to talk. The physical exhaustion connected with the care, maintenance, feeding and watering of the horses went on and on. The enemy was reported to be only 20 miles away, but how could we fight in this condition? I knew I could not.

At 9:00 that evening orders were given to camp for the night in a nearby field. Immediately everybody felt better. At least we might have a chance to stretch out and get those heavy riding boots off for a few hours. We were too tired to even think of cooking something hot. Bread was enough. At 3 a.m. the bugler blew the alarm and our wonderful rest suddenly was over. A British brigade, just recently shipped to Antwerp under orders of the First Sea Lord, Winston Churchill, was reported to be making a sortie and our division had to stop it. Our battery had to proceed quickly to Campenhaut near Macheln, about 15 miles south of Antwerp on the road to Brussels.

To get a battery ready to march at 3 a.m. when it was still pitch dark was no easy matter. First I had to take care of my horse. Where do I find a bucket of clear water? Where is the man who gives out the feed? I admit I was clumsy. I was barely ready when the battery commander gave the signal to march. Somebody had brewed some coffee over an open fire, but I had no time to get near it. I ate some dry bread while the battery was clattering along the highway.

We found ourselves amidst lots of soldiers — infantry, cavalry and more artillery all were marching toward Antwerp. British cavalry patrols had been sighted ahead, so we heard. The weather was hot and dry and after numerous stops we arrived near Macheln in the early afternoon. The battery commander rode forward to find a good position for our six guns and he ordered me to ride with him as an interpreter. We found a good open field and the battery was ordered to take up a firing position. This was done at leisure as no firing could be heard anywhere. Just behind us was a tall smoke stack of some factory. A staff officer had it blown up because he thought it would help the British to zero in on our battery.

Orders were given to dig in and erect earthworks on the side of the guns to protect us from small arms fire. In front of us, about 300 yards away, the infantry was digging in. The whole division was spread out in a huge semi-circle. It was hoped the British would be trapped in this loop and be mowed down from three sides.

By nightfall all orders had been executed, but we were told our supply wagon with the bread and meat was lost somewhere. I still had a little dry bread in my pocket. By now the thought of a really nice, hot meal with plenty of meat and potatoes became almost an obsession. In front of us were houses and I wondered if I could find something there to eat. We tried, but they were empty.

The overall situation was quite peaceful and I was content except for the fact I was terribly hungry for something solid to eat. Perhaps once asleep, the hunger would go away. The bugler blew a roll call and to my utter disgust I had guard duty that night. As a private first class I had three soldiers under me who actually would stand guard, taking turns every two hours. Between turns they could sleep, but I was not allowed to sleep all night. I had to check the men to see they were at their posts and awake. In peacetime I had done this quite often and I knew my duties, but how could I remain awake all night long as tired as I was? In peacetime, one night without sleep was managable, but I was ready to drop before the night had even started. How I passed that night and managed not falling asleep I will never quite know. I was terribly afraid I might doze off and several times I did, only to wake up suddenly in terror. Had somebody seen me asleep? Sleeping on guard duty before the enemy could be punished by death. An officer was supposed to check on me, but he never came. We were rather well trained in this guard duty business. In our home garrison of Fritzlar we had to guard a stone tower containing our live ammunition. Once, while standing guard at night, I saw a figure creeping toward me in the grass. I knew it was one of the officers testing whether I knew all the rules. I was supposed to warn him three times before shooting and there had to be a proper and correct time interval between each shouted warning. I did all that and just before the last warning the fellow would disappear. Of course, the officers would never admit they tested us that way. We had to make a long written report, but I could never believe that any person would want to blow up the tower.

I was glad when the next morning dawned. Nothing had happened all night long. Once in a while I heard some rifle fire and some bullets came whining over, but I believe it was our own infantry firing at shadows. During the afternoon orders came to march toward Termonde where a British force of some strength had been seen. We were told the British were trying to retake Brussels.

That night we had fine quarters on a huge estate — a castle-like house surrounded by a park with a beautiful lake. After the guns and all the horses were lined up for the night, an elderly woman, walking with a cane, came out of the big house raising hell and shouting at some nearby soldiers. I translated to our commander that this lady was complaining because some of our men had trampled her rose bed. Our lieutenant was a gentleman. He raised himself up in his stirrups and threatened dire consequences to any soldier not respecting this lady's rose garden.

For the first time since we crossed the Belgian border we had a good night's sleep with enough food. Our spirits rose. War was not too bad after all. Nobody had been hurt yet. We heard the German armies in France had won tremendous victories and that Paris might fall in a few days. There was a good chance this war might be over real soon. At that time I had daydreams about getting out of this bothersome war and instead going to a fine restaurant to order double portions of everything on the menu.

The next day we marched through Brussels which seemed undamaged. The weather was extremely hot. The sight of normal looking streets and people cheered us up and the many good looking stores and restaurants quickly aroused desires we had all but forgotten. Maybe we could pick up some nice things to eat and drink.

At the first stop I was ordered to report to the battery commander who was riding at the head of the battery. All the officers were with him and as I arrived they quickly explained they wanted me to go ahead and buy them all the goodies I could find. Money was to be no object and two men were ordered to go with me. Bicycles were produced and off we went. Brussels was firmly in German hands I was told, but at the same time, we were warned not to get off the main highway. I had not ridden a bicycle for many years and my heavy long boots with spurs, plus the revolver with an oversized wooden holster, were quite a handicap.

Looking around I could not see a single German soldier, although we had now penetrated to what I thought must be the main business section of Brussels. Evidently no fight had taken place here, no buildings were burning and no white flags were hanging out of windows. Maybe we were the only soldiers on such a forage mission. That did not seem plausible. Something had to be wrong.

On the right side of the broad avenue I saw one of those smallish, elegant looking stores which, in normal times, might sell fine candies, caviar and other imported food. The show window seemed full of stuff. So I waved to my men to wait outside while I went in. Inside were two nice and very clean looking sales girls, frightened to death. They told me to take anything I wanted, but leave them alone. Of course, I must have looked filthy and the enormous .45 at my side looked threatening to them. It took me some time to calm them down enough to have a more or less normal conversation. I showed them my money and assured them everything would be paid for. We were the first German soldiers they had seen nearby. I asked their permission to go behind the counter and take what we wanted from the shelves. This I did while the women cowered in the corner, wondering what would happen to them next. Finally I had selected quite a pile of foodstuffs, ranging from caviar and canned meats to imported English cookies. Now, how much would all this cost? They didn't know or care. Finally they pulled themselves together and added everything up. It came to about 200 marks, or $50, which I paid. My two soldiers had little baskets, but all this stuff would have filled 10 baskets.

The battery might come up at any time, but how were we to transport all of this? One of the girls suggested hiring a horse-drawn passenger cab and that proved to be a very good solution. We had no trouble finding one. I explained to the driver that he had to wait in one of the side streets until our battery came by, then he should drive alongside it until we could unload while marching. It was difficult to imagine how this unloading would proceed and where we would stow it all, but it was the best I could think of. To park the vehicle on the main highway might attract the attention of some staff officer. We did not want to be arrested for looting.

After half an hour the battery showed up and it was astonishing to see how quickly everything was gobbled up and stowed away. One of the officers took charge of it and everybody seemed pleased, except the driver of the cab who now wanted his money. I signaled him to drive to the curb where I followed on my bicycle. The sum he asked for was absolutely outrageous. He argued about the risks he had taken, etc., all of which made no sense to me. I knew we used his cab for about two hours so I paid him what a two-hour cab trip in Bremen would have cost.

As a sort of reward I now belonged to the battery staff as interpreter and horse holder. The staff was mounted beautifully, except me. The top sergeant disliked one-year men, and I was the worst of them in his opinion, so he gave me a poor horse. It was easy to get on or off, but was too small and unable to canter with any speed. To complain about it would have been useless.

Baptism by fire

After marching through Brussels we went west toward Alost-Termonde where we received our baptism of fire. We knew nothing of the overall military situation near us, but evidently we were deep in enemy territory and that must be a good sign.

Part of the division was somewhere else. Our battle group consisted of our six-gun battery and the 84th and 163rd Infantry regiments. We marched through Termonde without trouble, but I noticed something was brewing. Cavalry patrols would come and go and staff officers in cars were speeding along the road. We were told not to start cooking. About noon the battery was ordered to march and as we came to what I thought were the outskirts of Termonde, the signal was given to go into firing position in a field already explored by the battery commander. We did this at full gallop and very shortly each gun reported ready. The battery had lost a few men through sickness and I was ordered to replace the Nr. 3 man on one of the guns. Number 3 was the man who gave the rough direction by swinging the gun trail right or left, and who set the distance at which the shell must explode with a special key. He had to listen carefully to the commands coming from the battery commander and which were repeated by the three officers each commanding and supervising the actions of two guns. In action these three officers were a few steps behind their two guns, kneeling. They had no cover. The crews did have some protection behind the steel shields across the gun barrels.

The men did their jobs quietly. Naturally we were apprehensive, but nobody showed fear. In fact, nobody knew exactly what to be afraid of. This was the first time we were exposed to real danger, but the man who is optimistic by nature, and I was one of them, always feels rather certain he will come out of it in good shape. I don't believe the thought of soon being dead or badly wounded came to any of us.

Now we heard infantry fire and the first command, "Artillery to the right of the small forest in front of us. Shrapnel, 2,400 yards. Fire one gun!"

It was just like peacetime maneuvers: Get the range with one gun and then plaster the enemy fast with all you've got. Several more rounds were fired. It seemed the commander did not yet have the right wind correction as we were not quite on target. I made myself as small as possible and had no desire to lift my head to look at our enemy. As long as our Nr. 1 man at the sights saw the enemy, that was sufficient. The first shrapnels were coming back toward us. Now we were really in a war. Those people on the other side were trying to kill us. It seemed incredible to me.

At first the enemy, whoever he was — Belgian, British or perhaps French — was shooting badly. His shrapnels were exploding some 200 yards in front of us and much too high. They made no more noise than firecrackers and hit nothing. It seemed we had the range; all guns were firing at medium speed, but perhaps we were not on target after all because enemy shells were now coming over thick and fast. Shrapnel bullets and splinters zooming through the air hit our shield with a frightening noise. Shells were exploding just to the right, in front of and behind the guns. We were dueling with an enemy artillery outfit of about the same caliber as ours. I can testify that the terrific noise and flash of the explosion of an ordinary 75 mm. or 77 mm. gun near you is a most terrifying and shattering experience. It is completely overwhelming and unbearable. But inspite of it all the battery worked well. We gave salvo for salvo and stretcher bearers carried away the first too be wounded.

The sergeant of my gun was a good friend of mine. He was a few years older, an easy-going sort of big fat boy who belonged to my rowing club. I saw blood dripping from his uniform when he told me he was hit. He said he did not want to leave us if I would remove the bullet which now seemed to hurt him very much. The shrapnel bullet was right under the skin and he handed me his pocket knife, telling me to go ahead and cut it out. I couldn't do it, nor did I have the time. I was glad when they carried him away. Six years later — in 1920 — I visited him in Stockholm where he was active in the lumber business.

This engagement lasted no more than 30 minutes or so. My diary does not say how many were wounded, but I remember that our losses were very light. After a man was hit he could count on being picked up by stretcher bearers rather quickly. These men were courageous soldiers, darting in and out whenever there was a chance. To carry a wounded man at a fast clip, half running for 100 yards or so, was no easy job.

But the battery had one unexpected victim. During the engagement one of the reserve officers had left his post. In his charge were the two guns on the right wing and it was his duty to remain between the guns. When the battery commander looked down from the steel ladder on which he was directing the action, he could not see this officer and thought he had been killed and carried away. To his astonishment he suddenly reappeared. The man had taken cover behind a stone pile just a few yards from his guns. The next morning he was sent home. Nobody knew what happened to him and no one talked about it.

During this action, when I thought the enemy had our range, it seemed to me we should have changed position. Had the enemy changed to shells instead of continuing to fire shrapnels, we would have had crippling losses. A shell, exploding on contact, fills the air with heavy pieces of metal. Hitting a few yards from a gun the pieces easily would penetrate the protective shield. When I thought the danger was greatest the signal was given to stop firing and to our amazement, fewer shrapnels were coming our way. It took us a few minutes to get accustomed to this sudden change when, through the din, we heard the infantry bugle call the attack, four simple notes repeated over and over again. It was a spine-tingling sound known to every German soldier and it meant now or never. How this attack fared we didn't know. We were too tired to care. When our infantry attacked the enemy battery had to switch its attention from us to the men moving toward them.

We now had time to catch our breath when I was called to report to the battery commander. He told me that during the last phase of the fight, while standing on the observation ladder, he saw bullets splattering on the protective shield from the rear. He believed partisans had fired on him from a house he showed me, about 150 yards behind us. Since I spoke French he thought I could find out what was going on. I could do nothing but click my heels, salute and say "Jawohl," although I had no idea exactly what was expected of me. There were so many houses within rifle range. If partisans really had taken some potshots at us they had ample time to hide their guns and look very harmless.

As we reached the house the door was wide open. Inside were only old people and a little girl, all appearing placid and completely calm. I received no answers to my questions at all. Nobody said one word. In fact, I could not think of an intelligent question to ask. Surely they would not say "yes" to a question whether anyone had fired a rifle from this house. We could not find anything suspicious and after hanging around for 10 minutes or so, we left. It was possible these people only spoke Flemish. I was happy they did not force me to take some sort of action because I would not have known what to do with those old people.

That same night we slept at the guns. The weather was warm, the enemy seemed far away and I slept quite well.

The next day, September 5, orders were given to clean up, get all equipment in top-notch shape, make minor repairs and receive replacements in men and horses. Inspection would be held that evening. It was a full day of very hard work. Our uniforms had to be clean, no mud on the shoes and horses and gear had to be spotless. To me it was quite an ordeal.

On September 6 we had a religious service in a nearby church and that meant appearing dressed up and on our best behavior. The division chaplain was too much of a firebrand for my taste. "Don't pray while you are shooting, you can't shoot straight if you do," seemed to be his main theme. According to this fellow, all of us had been leading nice, peaceful lives when the rest of the world, without rhyme or reason, suddenly jumped us to steal the fruits of our labors. Most of us tried to get a little sleep, but I got the gist of his sermon.

Antwerp was one of the most modern fortresses, equipped with some very heavy guns distributed among the several forts defending the approaches. Field artillery had no role to play in the coming fight about Antwerp and we were ordered to march toward Ghent.

For several days I had been feeling quite bad. Since we had crossed the border on August 25, my stomach had been mistreated violently. For fear of perhaps finding no food at all the next day, we were forever stuffing ourselves whenever we had the chance. But the trouble was we ate everything — fresh meat just slaughtered before our eyes, well cooked or half cooked, any kind of bread, fresh or stale. It was still the business of each gun crew to prepare its own meals. And it was imperative to fill one's canteen early in the morning. If we were close to a house with running water, or had some leftover coffee, no problems would arise. But sometimes we had to take water out of the nearest little stream and we had no idea if it was clean or contaminated. In some abandoned houses we found wine which we used for drinking. At any rate, I felt ill and apparently looked it because the lieutenant ordered me to get a good night's sleep in a large building nearby. Nobody knew what it was. But the idea that I might find a real bed inside seemed to good to be true. Later on I learned the building had been a monastery, but now was being used as an insane asylum.

The inhabitants were friendly and received me well. I could see they belonged to some kind of male Catholic order. After explaining I felt sick and would like to sleep in a bed, they were most cooperative in a silent sort of way. I could wash, take off my clothes and soon feel like a human being. They brought me milk and I locked the door. I had been warned because nobody knew who was a partisan fighter and who was not. Someone would have to break down the door before they could reach me so I felt quite safe and wonderfully comfortable in a clean bed between white sheets. I put my pistol under the pillow and the only fear I had was that the battery might have to move during the night, forgetting me and leaving me behind with all those Belgians. But nothing at all unusual happened.

Nach Paris

On September 11 news reached the battery to get ready for a long march to Paris by forced marches. No newspapers were available and rumors were wild. If Paris had been taken, maybe we would be serving as occupation troops. That would be wonderful. One of the Bremen boys who I knew well had been a portrait painter in Paris when the war had broken out. He hoped to find his studio in fine shape for a big party. We all looked forward to a good time. But in reality, things were vastly different from our dreams.

By September 6, Germany's armies had reached the Marne River, about 75 miles from Paris which had been evacuated by the French government. Tremendous victories had been won, but the French-English armies refused to collapse.

Our enemies fought brilliantly with the utmost tenacity and courage. They gave ground only after inflicting terrible losses, making counter-attacks whenever possible. When it appeared impossible to beat the French-English armies by clever maneuvers, the German High Command substituted a plan of ruthless, ceaseless attack, hoping to smash and pulverize enemy resistance.

While these bloody battles were being fought, France and England sent frantic messages to their Russian ally, urging the Russians to attack immediately. This the Russians did. They overran the East Prussian border finding only weak resistance. The situation for Germany was now truly desperate. At this critical moment two army corps had to be transferred from the Western Front to hold back the invading Russians.

The French High Command detected the weakness caused by this withdrawal and quickly threw its last reserves into the battle on the Marne. The famed Paris taxis were loaded with troops and rushed to the battlefield where overtired German troops could not hold back this fresh onslaught. It was reported that at first glance it was impossible to determine whether the many German infantrymen lying on the ground were dead or just sleeping. Later on, so-called experts expressed the view that one day's rest would have refreshed the German soldiers sufficiently to have taken Paris.

One contributing factor to this French-English defensive victory was the effectiveness of their excellently led field artillery. The French 75 mm. field gun could fire up to 12,000 yards while our maximum range was only 7,500 yards. Frequently our infantry had to attack merely to bring our artillery into range. The French stayed carefully out of range, inflicting fearful losses with their accurate fire.

That was the situation by the middle of September. The German armies had to retreat to a position still deep in enemy territory, which they held for the next four years. It was a very dangerous retreat, requiring the utmost discipline to avoid an enemy breakthrough which might have occurred at any time. A fresh French colonial army now appeared on the battlefield, shipped from North and West Africa, and was led by French officers. They were thrown into the battle and tried to change our retreat into a rout. We didn't know it then but our 9th Reserve Corps was the only one left to hold this French counterattack mounted by fresh troops. They fought us in their gaudy peacetime uniforms — red and white Zouave pants and blue coats.

The attacking German combat troops on the Western Front originally numbered roughly one million men. By September 15, 1914, we had lost two-thirds of our officers and two-fifths of the men, dead and wounded.

On our way to the Marne battlefield we marched south toward the Belgian-French border. Whenever the lieutenant was afraid of partisan activities he ordered me to cover the flank of the battery by moving on a road parallel to the main road, or, if there was no suitable road, I had to ride in the fields some 200 feet to the right. It was an uncomfortable job to ride toward a cluster of civilians standing on the road, wondering if they might shoot. My greetings were always friendly, but I never received a reply. I had a very poor horse and that worried me. It could not run or jump.

The weather was hot. The division was on the road before dawn and we marched all day. When we got to Valenciennes in France it so happened that our battery stopped in the suburbs. Soon a French housewife began a conversation and I explained to her that we were very hungry and were looking for a place to cook a meal. Would she permit us to cook on her stove? She offered to cook for us if we furnished the meat. That woman cooked an excellent meal. She invited us into her house and we ate at her table, covered with a white tablecloth. She was the motherly type and we thanked her profusely, paying for the potatoes and vegetables she had furnished.

For the first time we saw enemy airplanes flying about 2,000 yards high and barely visible against the light blue sky. One would appear just before sundown and cruise leisurely over our bivouac area. It seemed every rifle of the division opened up on him without having the slightest effect. Artillery guns could not elevate sufficiently and it looked as if nothing could prevent the flier from seeing where we were. The plane was of the "Taube" (dove) type, a single-decker with a 100-horsepower motor. At that time planes were used exclusively for reconnaissance, but as a side line they also dropped steel arrows and hand grenades. The whole division was camped below and the airman could not miss. While he was circling over us we took cover under the

gun and only after he left did we dare go sleep in our tents. Seven arrows penetrated the tent of a neighboring gun crew. An arrow would go
through a standing horse with ease. This flier also threw the first bomb
I ever saw. The crater was only a few inches deep, but his 800-gram
bomb thrown by hand could kill anybody standing close by. Nobody
took these planes very seriously, but at the same time, they created
fear because they seemed untouchable.

At the outbreak of the war France was the leader in military aviation. French fliers had made international headlines and already they
knew how to fly at night. By the end of 1912, for instance, the French
army had 234 personnel who could fly, while the German army had only
50 fliers. The Germans put their money into zeppelins. The first bombing attack was made by the French on August 9, 1914, using bombs
weighing 4½, 10, 20 and 50 kilograms. Against ground troops the French
were using a 12-kilo bomb which burst into 1,400 pieces. However, fliers
and bombing attacks were still quite rare and the damage done was
negligible. At that time nobody could guess that before the end of the
war the skies literally would swarm with them.

While on this march to the Marne battlefield all kinds of rumors
reached us. So far we had received mail and newspapers only once. We
knew that victory or defeat hung in the balance, but the people at home
seemed to be fooled by the large amounts of enemy territory already
occupied by our armies. That fact alone did not spell victory and the
end of the war. France and England still were fighting fiercely and
were not close to collapse as imagined by the newspapers I read.

Anything over 15 miles per day was called a forced march. We covered about 20 miles and that was obviously too much for the infantry.
After a few hours of marching the ditches would fill up with soldiers
too tired to go one more step. A few weeks before they had been civilians and this was just too much for them. A full pack and rifle must
have been an awful load in those hot summer days. After riding a few
hours I would prefer to march next to my horse, but marching in my
high riding boots was not much relief either. One day I was used as a
riding messenger after we had entered bivouac and my diary says I
was 17 hours in the saddle that day.

At times my upset stomach made me quite weak and after taking
care of my horse at night I was utterly exhausted and desperately long-
ing for an end to this miserable existence.

My official regimental record says I participated in the "Battle of
Noyon," which lasted from September 17-25 and was a phase, probably
the last one of the so-called battle of the Marne. The whole affair was a
nightmare.

The battle of Noyon

On September 16, near the town of Noyon, we were told to get ready
for battle. Noyon is situated about 25 miles south of the Somme River.

French and English troops were reported massing for another attack from the direction of Amiens, some 45 miles to the northwest of us. The German troops were overextended; several divisions had been sent to the Eastern Front to stop the advancing Russians and a decisive French-English victory was now possible. After weeks of bloody fighting on French soil, the French general staff was now ready for the big counterpush which would destroy the invader.

That same afternoon we approached the battlefield and the constant noise of artillery fire ahead told us we must be near the front lines. We were in a dense forest when a halt was ordered and this seemed to be a good chance for a little nap. The infantry in front and behind us was eating. Orders came through to feed the horses, too, which was done by removing the bits and hanging a canvas feedbag over the horses' heads. The whole scene was a peaceful one. Perhaps we could sleep tonight in these nice woods.

Suddenly, and literally out of the blue sky, salvo after salvo of French 75 mm. shells and shrapnel slammed into our troops. The infantry scattered deeper into the woods to the sides of the road where they found good cover behind the trees. But our guns and horses were bound to the road. There was no escape. Within seconds horses were hit. We tried to hold them, but had only the feedbags to hold them with. The exploding shells and shrapnel made an awful, frightening noise and it seemed we were completely defenseless. The infantry saw our plight and helped us. We had to clear the road or the French artillery would destroy us before we entered the battle. We went to work with heavy axes (we had two for every gun), cutting out the dead horses and leading the wounded and healthy ones into the woods. Medics took care of the wounded men, but we had to struggle with the animals. Finally we collected the remaining horses some 50 yards off the road. Twenty-six horses were dead or wounded and had to be replaced immediately. They arrived late that night, but without harnesses. It took hours of very hard work to harness up these new animals. And it had to be done at night, without proper lights.

Our division, consisting of four regiments of infantry, two regiments of artillery, cavalry and supply wagons, was entirely horsedrawn. The column was 16 miles long and probably had been spotted by a French plane. It was easy for the French artillery to keep its fire on the road. We could not escape. After letting us have it they switched their fire further back on the road and everybody was wondering why we were so jammed in. Why could we not move forward?

The middle rider on our gun was one of those wounded and to my amazement I was ordered to take his place, a job for which I had no training whatever. I never had ridden a horse pulling a gun — that was no place for an officer candidate. It took two years of daily peacetime training to make a combat-ready middle rider, who had to control the horse he was riding and manage the other horse pulling the gun on his right side as well. But controlling two bucking horses during the noise and confusion of battle was a mean job. If it was not done right there would be confusion and the crew would be exposed to enemy fire longer than necessary while galloping the guns into firing position. My right wrist was tender and thin, suitable for playing the violin, but most unfit for a middle rider. I was afraid I could not hold these two horses and that I might endanger the lives of the rest of the crew. If everything went slowly I would manage allright.

Fortunately we went into position without enemy interference and at a slow trot. I was relieved and happy when a replacement arrived — one of those big German farm boys who seemed happy and competent around horses and who had a wrist as big as my arm.

Orders were given to throw up earthworks for our protection, but later that afternoon a change of position was executed without enemy interference. It began to rain hard and soon we were soaked, although our heavy overcoats seemed to repel the rain pretty well. Our skins still were dry and so were our feet. When night came we found the ground a sea of mud on which no tent could be erected. All night long we tried to doze standing or leaning against the gun or a horse. Before dawn we had some hot black coffee which made me feel a little better. It still rained. We could not feel more miserable.

As the sun came up we wondered what would happen next. In front of us, maybe five miles away, the noise of battle was going full blast, but the rain and wind made it difficult to determine by ear exactly what was going on. What were we doing here several miles behind the fighting lines? Much later we learned that the German divisions in front of us were retreating slowly toward our position. Our division received the retreating troops so they could reform behind our position which was to be held at all costs. Our division represented the only fresh troops our High Command could throw in to stop the retreat and avoid a disaster. The French were supposed to be equally exhausted, but the German High Command did not know that the first French colonial troops had arrived the night before. They were now massed for their first battle in the forest of Compiegne, clearly visible right in front of us, only a few thousand yards away.

Orders reached the battery to bombard the woods ahead of us and we opened up at 4,200 yards. Whether it was French heavy or light artillery that hit us in response I don't know, but the RRhum-WWhang and the fire and flash of their shells was terrifying. Whenever one came awfully close one could not help but shudder. The ground was wet and soft and the craters deep, directing many of the steel splinters upward. But a direct hit on the gun barrel would have finished us right quick. The lieutenant still was standing on his steel observation ladder and I wondered how long he could remain there without being hit by splinters now zooming around in all directions. But that man did not panic. In fact, nobody did. The night before a new lieutenant of the reserve had arrived to command our two right-wing guns. He came from Hamburg and seemed very nice. I admired his new tailormade officer's uniform.

Just a few minutes after the first enemy shells came over, a splinter hit him and he was lying a yard from our gun, crumpled up, holding his stomach with his hands and bleeding profusely. It shook me up to see him lying there helpless and I wished the medics would come. They finally arrived, but later I heard he died.

Shortly after we began this long-range artillery duel, our own heavy artillery behind us opened up and we hoped they were firing on the guns still firing at us with great accuracy. This went on for about half an hour. What our losses were I didn't know, but our battery kept up a steady fire. I was Nr. 3 at our gun and it was my job to give the rough direction whenever a change of target was ordered. Around my neck I carried the large key-like tool which I used to set the distance on the shrapnel head for the shrapnel to explode. I had to listen carefully to the commands coming from the battery commander.

Suddenly, for the first time, I noticed alarm in his voice. He was almost shrieking: "Change target! Shrapnel! Infantry attacking us coming out of the woods, 2,400 yards!"

There was no time to zero in first with one gun. The enemy had to be stopped. Where was our infantry? How could the enemy infantry be attacking us? First they had to overrun our own men fighting in front of us somewhere. But we did not know then that our infantry practically had been wiped out the night before. There was nobody between us and the troops now attacking — French colonial infantry, Zouaves, Moroccans, Senegalese and part of the Foreign Legion.

It was alarming to notice we steadily were reducing the firing distance. We started at 2,400 yards. Now the enemy was at 1,500 yards. He was running toward us or we were shooting badly. I heard the commander shouting something to the effect he had lost the target or could not see it. We wondered why. Was he wounded? A sergeant of the right-wing gun sensed something was amiss. The order to stop firing had been given despite the fact infantry bullets still were zinging all around us, sounding like hundreds of chirping birds, many hitting our protective shield. The sergeant climbed a high tree nearby as fast as a cat and shouted he could see the enemy only 500 yards in front of us, still coming. For his resolute action he received the first Iron Cross second class given to our battery.

All guns were now at rapid fire, point-blank, 250 yards, mixing shrapnel and shell. We could see the bursts and the mud and debris flying into the air, but not the enemy. At that rate of firing we needed ammo quickly and hoped the lieutenant commanding the six ammo wagons knew the situation. Later on we heard a messenger from the battery had ordered the wagons to come forward at whatever cost, and that same messenger had orders to report to the infantry commander that the battery would be overrun soon unless supported by machine-guns.

I was now detached from my gun under orders to keep track of our ammo supply and report to the commander how much was left. It was impossible to run from gun to gun and count the shells so I ran to the

middle gun, counted its ammo and multiplied by six. We were very
short — that was obvious — and the order was given to stop firing when
we saw our ammo wagons dashing up at full speed toward us. They
were supposed to unload the ammo within reach of the gun crews, but
they never got that far. The French clearly must have seen them because it seemed no trouble to shoot off the riders and after that it was a
jumble of kicking horses and wounded men. But the wagons were un-
hooked and left on the field about 30 feet behind our guns. Everybody
ran over and grabbed two ammo baskets, each containing three shells
— a heavy load to drag over mud for 30 feet. We did not dare run upright, but sort of crawled in the mud the best we could. For the next 10
minutes or so only half the crew kept up the point-blank fire while the
rest lugged the ammo, all the time hoping some help would come from
somewhere. To the right of us I suddenly noticed 20 or 30 horses, all
riderless, running around aimlessly and frightened by the noise.
French cavalry had tried to overrun the battery on our right flank, but
did not succeed.

The turning point then came just at the right moment. It seemed we
had stopped the attack because we were ordered to "Fire slowly."
Everybody breathed easier when we saw from behind a machine-gun
company running at the double toward our battery. The guns were set
up between our wheels and blazed away at the enemy, still very close.
The din of battle was earsplitting, but we knew that with these machine-guns the French could never overrun us. What exactly broke the
enemy attack I don't know, but to our surprise, firing stopped and
somebody shouted, "Look, there they are!" For the first time I could
see the enemy, streaming back like ants over the open field and up a
little hill some 500 yards away. They left their dead and wounded lying
on the ground, their white-gray baggy pants plainly visible. Zouaves
from Morocco. All fighting in our sector had stopped.

The battery was in a mess. Our ammo wagons had been shot up and
we had lost men and officers. Medics swarmed all over the place taking away the wounded or holding mirrors in front of the mouths of
doubtful cases. If the mirror did not fog up, the man was dead and left
there.

For the time being we were not combat ready and to our delight, we
were ordered to leave the battlefield and go into quarters somewhere.
Our billets were supposed to be in the small town of Carlepont, but as
we entered we found it overcrowded with French prisoners standing
around in groups, talking and smoking. Nobody paid any attention to
these prisoners of war. It was an astonishing sight to suddenly see the
enemy so close by in uniform. It seemed they all belonged to African
regiments and still wore their peacetime uniforms. The officers and
non-commissioned officers looked white, the Moroccans brown and the
Senegalese pitch black — their faces disfigured with deep gashes inflicted in childhood as a tribal custom. It was a peaceful scene. They
just stood around and whenever a German soldier approached with

food or to give directions, both sides were anxious to be polite. Soon, friendly conversations between Germans and French were going on everywhere. Carlepont was filled with several thousand French prisoners.

Solid quarters could not be found anywhere and we were forced once more to go into bivouac. By this time I was so tired and worn out I really did not care much about anything. Just let me sleep. After taking care of my horse, thinking this horrible day had finally come to an end, I heard the top sergeant call my name. I knew he still disliked me and felt I had to do something unpleasant. Only a few days before I overheard the battery commander describe this sergeant as a "coward and a bully." Whatever happened, I knew he would not be able to give me a black eye with our commander. But I still had to obey.

He ordered me to take two men with a wagon, go back to where our ammo wagons had been shot up, and salvage the equipment off the dead horses. It was still raining lightly. The night was dark as pitch and it took us quite a while before we reached our old position. We had no lights and the only illumination came from a few burning houses on the edge of the field. When we came across a cluster of what looked like dead horses in the dark, we groped with our hands across the cadavers to find the heads first. We took off a few harnesses, but when we tried to loosen the belts holding the saddles, none of us had strength enough to do it. The horses' bellies were extended; legs and mouths were stiff as boards and we soon found it useless to salvage worthwhile equipment. If it had not rained I believe we would have collapsed right there. But it was impossible to think of sleep in that mud. Against the burning houses we could see men wandering on the battlefield and we wondered what they were doing. Were they friends or enemies? Occasionally, some bullets could be heard zipping through the air, but otherwise it was quiet.

It was about 10 p.m. when we got back to Carlepont. With the rain, sleeping in bivouac again was an unpleasant thought. I was afraid of sleeping in the open because several nights running I had been sleepwalking, suddenly waking up yards away from my tent, having no idea where I was. A few times I was unable to find my tent and all I could do was squat down and wait for the day to come. There seemed to be plenty of houses in Carlepont and I was determined to get a roof over my head this time. When I saw a sentry in front of what appeared to be a large building, I asked the soldier whether there was room for me to sleep. He said there were a few hundred black prisoners inside and if I could find room he had no objections to my sleeping there. When I opened the door I saw two German infantrymen sitting on a table in the middle of the room, back to back, their rifles at the ready. A candle between them gave off a very dim light. The floor was covered completely with sleeping Senegalese soldiers. I pushed the soldier sleeping close to the door with my foot to make room and in a few minutes I was fast asleep.

The battle of Roye

We had two days rest during which time the battery had to be made combat ready again. Replacements in men and horses arrived as well as warm food. Then orders came to clear the woods near the town of Roye. Our battery was to support the attacking infantry.

As the infantry attack developed, we were waiting behind a small hill when I saw a small plane landing nearby, evidently bringing a message to the commanding general who had his command post close to our battery. What was going on in front of us we didn't know. Enemy artillery was not bothering us, but lots of rifle bullets were zinging over our heads, though much too high to hit us. Only a spent bullet could reach us behind the little hill. After some more waiting, a liaison officer brought the message that our infantry had entered the woods in front of us, but could not proceed further without artillery support. He also reported enemy infantry had taken to the trees from where they were inflicting severe losses among our men who could not see them in the dense foliage. It became our job to blast them out of the trees. This was a new type of warfare for which we had not been trained.

No enemy could be seen when we entered the woods, but judging from the bullets flying around everywhere, the enemy was much in evidence. Our battery was now in imminent danger of being crippled by rifle fire, so the guns were ordered out of the woods. An infantry colonel explained the situation in detail to our lieutenant and shortly thereafter we were shooting at the treetops from a range of some 1,200 yards, hoping to bring down the sharpshooters. The infantry was pleased with the results. This fight lasted all afternoon without causing losses among our men.

The next day our battery was ordered again to take position near Roye. For several hours we had to wait on a highway very close to a field hospital. The wounded were being brought in by stretcher bearers from every direction and it looked as if hundreds of them were waiting for the doctor to treat them. I wondered what would happen to these wounded if it started raining again. There were no tents, only a small farmhouse serving as an operating room. Once in a while we would see one of the surgeons with his bloody apron come out into the fresh air to take a rest and smoke a cigarette. Ambulances would come up and the medics would separate the dead from the wounded by the mirror method. My parents had sent me so-called "cola" pills which were supposed to help a soldier overcome severe emotional stress. I had forgotten all about these pills, but now I felt I needed at least a double dose. Whether they helped I cannot say, but I continued to feel I could not last much longer. Some of the other soldiers in our outfit looked undisturbed and unaffected by the things we had gone through since crossing the Belgian border. I decided they must have been much tougher than I was.

In hospital

The French were stopped from breaking through and no more big fights took place in our sector for the time being. These front lines remained roughly the same for four years. Now the race to the sea had started. The English army tried to outflank the German right wing in Belgium, resulting in very bloody battles in the fields of Flanders. But before winter, a stalemate had been reached everywhere on the Western Front. What next? Nobody knew. Peace by Christmas had only been a silly slogan.

On October 20 I reported sick. I was now so weak I could hardly stand up. It took the doctor just a few minutes to declare me unfit for combat. He said my heart was bad and that I might have cholera. I didn't care what I had, and when he ordered an ambulance to take me to the field hospital in Senceny, I felt happy and elated. I soon went to sleep on a stretcher, dreaming about sleeping again in white beds, taking baths, eating from plates and forgetting about this war. My spirits rose. The field hospital personnel were most anxious to please. Did I want anything? No, nothing. Just let me sleep.

The next day I arrived at the hospital for contagious diseases in Senceny, some 25 miles behind the front. I was carried into a large hall full of beds. A Catholic nun named Margarete was in charge of my bed. I was extremely comfortable and could sleep all day. The sister woke me up only to eat. After a few days of this I began to wonder and ask questions. I was told my heart had gone bad through overexertion; my pulse beat varied from 130 to 170 while lying in bed. In time, the doctor said, this probably would correct itself with rest. My condition was diagnosed as dysentery, not cholera. I was in the wrong hospital and would be transported to a hospital in Germany in a week or so. I now knew nothing much was the matter with me, though I never had heard of a "neurotic heart." It caused no pain or discomfort as long as they would let me lie in a comfortable bed.

The only one who disturbed me at night was a soldier in the bed next to me. He was 40 years old, thin and emaciated looking, with deep-set eyes. Sister Margarete would not tell me what was wrong with him, but insinuated he was going crazy. Quite a number of soldiers had lost their minds, I was told, and this fellow seemed to be one of them. At night he would shriek, stand up in bed and stretch out his long, thin arms in wild gestures until some orderlies rushed up and calmed him down. It seemed he was in the wrong hospital, too.

After two weeks I felt quite good, but the doctor ordered me sent to a hospital in Germany. In my compartment were seven French "infermiers" trained as hospital personnel to take care of the many French wounded on the train. They were taken prisoner while attending their wounded. All were well educated Frenchmen. One was studying for the priesthood.

Our trip to Saxony took two days. During this time our friendly conversations became quite animated. They were sure we had attacked the French nation without cause, but who was to blame? They didn't know. It was a catastrophe that had to be ended quickly, they argued, but how?

Finally our train arrived in Zwickau, the home of the well known Horch automobile works. At the depot hundreds of autos were ready to carry the wounded to the hospital. My French friends and I were loaded into a sedan driven by a fat man, who, to my astonishment, had a big revolver strapped to his hip. I didn't know what he expected to do with it. Later on I was told it was Herr Horch himself who drove us. He looked like a fat, scared rabbit to me. It was completely ridiculous to arm himself as protection against those wounded Frenchmen.

It was late before I got to bed. The male nurse offered me a big glass of milk and a ham sandwich and I never felt better in my life. From then on I was scheming to get home.

My father already had written to the authorities, offering to pay for a private doctor if I could be treated at home. This request was unusual, but because all hospitals were overfilled, his request was granted after some wrangling. My father came to Zwickau to get me and at the beginning of December 1914, I reached Bremen. Apparently my appearance shocked my family. I still wore the same uniform I went to war in four months before and by now it looked dirty and worn.

Our own doctor had been drafted and I was lucky to be under his care. Every few days he came to our house to check my pulse. Walking up and down the room a few times would bring the pulse beat up to 170 and I was unable to digest ordinary food properly. But after 45 days my heart and digestion were more or less normal again and I was declared fit for combat service with the proviso "needs consideration." They didn't know what my heart would do under great exertion.

A Rumpler Taube observation plane.

Belgian prisoners.

A common scene after a day's march during the German advance into France, 1914.

Nagel, in the uniform of the 45th Field Artillery, with his fiancee Dorothy Lane.

THREE

1915

A new assignment

In the beginning of January I was shipped to the barracks of the 45th Field Artillery Regiment at Bahrenfeld near Hamburg to await a new assignment. On January 23 I was assigned to the newly formed Flak Battery Nr. 54 (B.A.K.), consisting of two reworked, horsedrawn French guns. They were rebored to 77 mm. to fit our standard field artillery ammunition. The outfit consisted of 40 men, 30 horses and was commanded by Second Lieutenant of the Reserve Schroeder, who I knew in private life. He was 47 years old and had not been in uniform for some 20 years. The army considered him too old, but he volunteered anyway. By profession he was in the export business. I liked him very much and it was obvious that this job would be a very soft one. He needed my assistance and that, of course, made things comfortable for me. The rest of the outfit were ordinary soldiers — none had been in the war yet — and I was the only one to whom the lieutenant could talk in confidence. I was very content and considered myself extremely lucky.

By this time enemy fliers had become quite numerous. They attacked installations in the rear and in the absence of constant and alert artillery protection, managed to do considerable damage. Corps and divisional staffs quartered in some farmhouse were more or less defenseless against sudden bomb or machine-gun attacks. The enormous accumulations of all kinds of war materiel behind the fighting fronts offered lucrative targets to the bombers, which by now could drop bombs up to 1,000 kilograms.

Between August 1914 and December 1918, a total of 47,637 planes were built for the German army and navy, consisting of 150 different types made by 35 firms. By the spring of 1915 we already had the Fokker E I. fighter plane with a fixed machine-gun firing through the propeller. One of the first to fly this type was Lt. Boelcke, the famous fighter pilot. A little later the first double-seater with two motors made its appearance. Our first bombers were the Albatros, the Gotha and the AEG. Our enemies had made similar progress and almost before we knew it, the war in the air had become very important. The re-

connaissance plane soon became the eyes of the High Command instead of the cavalry, and the fighter plane had to shoot the enemy's
down. From this concept huge air battles developed. An offensive could
not be successful if enemy reconnaissance planes detected the accumu-
lation of ammunition and the movement of troops and trains toward the
front lines.

We were one of the very first anti-aircraft batteries formed, but nobody knew much about firing at airplanes and we had no idea what our
future role would be. The letters B.A.K. stood for Ballonabwehrkanon
— balloon defense cannon — and we therefore presumed the protection
of our observation balloons would be our main job. These huge balloons, floating almost defenseless in the sky, were ideal targets for
fighter planes, especially since it took almost an hour then to wind up
the steel rope by hand in bringing a balloon to the ground.

It was obvious we needed special training to fire our French guns. On
February 25, 1915, we were shipped to the Krupp target range at Tan-
gerhuette where Krupp engineers instructed us. We were shooting at
kite balloons and became quite efficient. Apparently our crew had been
selected with care. Among the men were excellent mechanics, carpen-
ters and all-around good and handy men, many of whom were married.
None of them ever gave us trouble and while a professional soldier
probably would have described us as a sloppy outfit, these men could
build or repair anything. Nobody got drunk or unruly. But in a parade
we would have made a poor showing. Nobody could do a decent gooses-
tep.

On March 3 our guns were loaded on flatcars and the outfit was shipped toward the Eastern Front. Until the very last moment we had no
idea where we would go, but as soon as I knew, I wired my family. They
were most unhappy and wired me to do everything possible to be trans-
fered to an outfit destined for the Western Front. The German people
thought that fighting the Russians was the worst fate a soldier could endure. They were barbarians, it was thought. Wounded German soldiers
were mutilated. They did not have enough doctors to take care of their
own wounded and disregarded civilized warfare. For me to make such
an appeal would have been ridiculous, quite apart from the fact I was
unwilling to leave this comfortable outfit. I could not imagine how
guarding a balloon could possibly land me in a Siberian salt mine as a
prisoner of war.

Furthermore, my personal equipment was of the best. My sleeping
bag was waterproof and well padded. What had made life so hard in
France was that so many things had to be done in the dark. Now I had a
big box of candles, plus matches. Just before we left Bahrenfeld I was
promoted to sergeant and was exempted from all physical work. I was
responsible for one gun and the crew. The general tone in the battery
was friendly and easy-going. Food was plentiful.

Nobody knew exactly where we were going, but soon we saw burned
out houses and realized we were in East Prussia, which had been occu-

pied by the Russians until a short time before. Red Cross stations were everywhere and the people did their utmost to supply us with smokes, food, wine and even money. One man threw a handful of folding money into our train compartment, declaring we were all heroes. He promised to give us more of the same as soon as we had killed more Russians. I believe he was crazy.

In talking to people who had gone through the Russian occupation I found that some of the reports about Russian behavior were true. However, some Russian outfits behaved very well. An owner of a large estate told me that the Russian officers quartered in his house had behaved like gentlemen and even gave tips to the servants.

But the overall situation on the Eastern Front was still dangerous in the extreme.

Life in Poland

When we arrived on the Eastern Front everything was relatively quiet. On the Western Front the German army was digging in. For more than two years it had to fight a defensive battle to keep the Allied armies from breaking through while we tried to knock out the huge Russian forces once and for all. A German offensive in the east was necessary to bolster the morale of the Austrian troops who were, at times, close to collapse. Back in Germany, fresh reserve divisions were formed and most of them were shipped to the east for the coming spring offensive. As we learned later, a huge encirclement of all Russian forces fighting on the German border was planned. But first we had to break through the front, which extended from the Baltic Sea to southern Galicia — some 900 miles. While German troops were marching to their positions, it was the job of all anti-aircraft batteries to prevent Russian reconnaissance planes from penetrating our lines and to keep their Sikorsky bombers from doing damage.

We arrived at the east German town of Allenstein and saw our first Russian soldiers, prisoners. They looked strong, well-dressed and stoical. I don't believe they knew where they were.

Also in Allenstein I saw for the first time a prince of the royal family of Hohenzollern. It was Prince Joachim, the youngest son of the Kaiser. He looked extremely stupid and had no chin.

Our first job was to protect the headquarters of the 20th Corps from bombing attacks. In March it was still bitter cold and windy on the Russian border. Once we had our two guns in position there was nothing to do but wait for an enemy plane to appear. Our position was in an open field. After loafing around the gun from sunup to sundown, we were almost frozen stiff. We spent the nights warm and comfortable in a nearby house.

The next day the commanding general of the 8th Army visited us. He was a tall, fine-looking, white-haired man, very friendly and polite. He wished us good luck.

During this early stage of the war we often had visitors from neighboring artillery outfits. They were astonished to see shells exploding high in the sky and had never heard of an anti-aircraft gun.

A few days later we were ordered to protect a heavy 21 cm. battery firing on one of the forts of the Russian fortress at Lomza, situated 25 miles from the Prussian border inside Poland (which belonged to Russia). This heavy battery was firing at a range of 12 miles. On the second day in this position we saw our first Russian plane. It came suddenly from behind, but managed to stay out of our range. The soldier managing the rangefinder thought we could reach him, so we fired two shots. An accident prevented firing more. One man at the gun got his finger caught in the recoil and we had to push the barrel back to free him. His finger was smashed. This was our first and only casualty.

According to the official record the siege of Lomza lasted until April 1915. During this time we had to change position frequently to protect various objects such as railroad depots, bridges and headquarters. Without anti-aircraft in the neighborhood it would have been easy to wipe out a division or corps staff with one well placed bomb. It was pure luck to hit an attacking plane, but we could place lots of exploding shells over a target. A few times a Russian ground attack was feared and in such cases we kept our horses nearby to pull out, if necessary. Nothing of that sort happened and we continued to lead the lives of rear echelon soldiers. After my experiences on the Western Front this comfortable life in Russia seemed too good to be true.

An enemy reconnaissance plane would come into range every few days. The pilot seemed to ignore our fire, never changing his course, and we wondered if our firing had any effect at all. There was no way to check whether the man operating the rangefinder was correct or not. And to correct the shooting by observation was a very tricky matter. From the ground it might look as if a shell had exploded just a few yards behind the target, but we could never tell if it had exploded too high or too low. A shell exploding 500 yards above the target could look like a near hit. We had a direct line to the corps headquarters we were protecting and sometimes somebody would call us up and explain we again had missed by a mile.

At the beginning of May the German forward movement began. One army attacked from the Baltic coast, the other from Galicia, and between the two it was hoped to catch and destroy the enormous masses of Russians, now fully mobilized and a constant threat to the German border. But the Russians gave ground, retreating more every day. They refused to be encircled.

Our outfit simply followed the advancing troops. Every day we would march from sunup to about 3 p.m., when we would go into position to protect headquarters. The weather was warm, sometimes hot, and while these marches were long, we still led a very comfortable life.

Food was plentiful and at night we could sleep soundly in our tents. Nothing at all worthwhile happened to us. Once in a while we were told some zeppelins would come over and to look for planes that might attack them.

Some days we would march through endless pine forests. Finally we came to the Bobr and Narew rivers where we took time out to have a fine swim and bathe our horses.

It must be admitted that our outfit did not look very military. Nobody ever came to inspect us or seemed to care what we did as long as we stuck close to corps headquarters, ready to protect it from anything unpleasant from above. Our men accumulated all kinds of junk which contributed to their comfort: cooking utensils, all sorts of baggage, even chairs could be seen dangling from our forage wagon. One of the wooden boxes belonged to me, containing such luxuries as good soap, clean shirts and plenty of nice things to eat sent by my family. It can be very hot in Russia. Some soldiers had their hats on, others rode bareheaded, some had opened their uniform collars, and what we could not stow away on the wagon was somehow tied to one of the guns. We looked like traveling gypsies until one fine day we saw a cluster of officers ahead of us on the side of the road, watching the division march by. Our lieutenant was riding in front smoking his big cigar when lightning struck. As we passed, a major of the General Staff came out of the group of high officers and asked the lieutenant what outfit we were. In his opinion we looked like bandits. He ordered us to clean up, put on our caps, close our collars and throw away all the junk. While riding beside us he shouted at us, asking, "What is that, and that .....?" Nobody dared to answer. One of the things offending him was a portable field toilet — a light chair from which the wicker seat had been removed.

This chewing out made us feel uncomfortable because only a few days before we had received a circular letter from army headquarters expressing the view that so far all Flak (B.A.K.) units in the army had proven useless. No hits had yet been recorded. We feared our pleasant existence might be terminated by transfer to some field artillery outfit.

During this offensive, which lasted until October 1915, we had contributed nothing to the great victories. Once in a while we would see a Russian flier and always hoped he would come within range so we could prove our usefulness. In July, Russian observation planes had become more numerous and according to my diary, on some days we fired 40 rounds or more.

In September heavy rains set in and the marching was very slow. Roads became groundless and every day one or both guns would get stuck in the deep mud, and that meant long delays. It took time to put an additional six horses in harness to pull out a gun from the mud, then up a hill.

On September 20 I was promoted to Offizierstellvertreter, the highest non-commissioned rank created during the war. I could now do officer's duty without actually being one. This rank was created especially for older non-commissioned officers who had some 15 years of army service and were capable of doing officer's field duty, but who, for lack of education and social reasons, could not be promoted with commissions. Now I could wear an officer's sword and hat, but not an officer's epaulets. It was my job to take charge when the lieutenant was absent, but in practice, there was very little to take charge of. Our men knew what to do and they did it willingly.

Whenever we marched through a Russian town, everybody seemed to be keyed up, hoping for some pleasant adventure. But these small country towns always were drab with absolutely nothing worthwhile to look at. Only a few civilians could be seen and we often wondered what had happened to the rest. My new rank entitled me to eat in the officers' messes. In Grodno and Lomsha there were excellent ones with good food and service, cold beer and shower baths. We lingered in those places as long as we could.

Outside Lomsha we had to protect our captive balloons, but no Russian fliers attacked. At the beginning of the war the balloons' maximum height was 1,500 feet, which was too low for useful observation. But soon new balloons were going up to 3,600 feet where they could stay and remain steady even in rough weather.

Our army had balloons in peacetime, but nobody then foresaw attacks by airplanes. It took one full hour to bring down these first balloons by hand-operated winches, and that was much too slow. Then, horses pulled them down, but now, the winches were driven by motors. Large numbers of these balloons appeared at the front, but we lacked qualified observers. Many front line infantry officers volunteered as observers, hoping for an easier life. Later on, beginning with the great battles on the Western Front in 1916, being a balloon observer became a nightmare. Balloons were under constant attack in good or bad weather and many observers had to jump several times a day to avoid being burned to death by a flaming balloon. An observer depended entirely upon the ground men to phone him when to jump; he had to keep his eyes on the enemy's ground forces. Broken clouds always invited enemy attacks. The observer could not jump just because an enemy plane was near. His man on the ground would let him do so only in case of an actual attack, and often the warning came too late. Not many men could take this constant parachute jumping for long and were glad to return to their old infantry outfits. Many were killed by the falling, burning balloon. One tracer machine-gun bullet from a plane could cause instant explosive destruction, but no observers were ever killed by malfunctioning parachutes, according to official records. The first parachutes were available by the end of 1915.

All of us now were suffering from lice. Whenever we saw a delousing station we took advantage of it. That helped for a little while. We hardly ever slept in a Russian farmhouse and could not understand where we had picked up these bugs. Once we had a visitor from a neighboring battery when I claimed to be free of lice for a change. I admitted to fleas, but I had killed all my lice. I lost a bet when he inspected my uniform collar. It was awful to see so many crawling around there. When we came close to a farmhouse I had no desire to sleep inside, but my men carried out a comfortable bed for me to sleep in. Fortunately, I carefully inspected it and found literally thousands of lice. At first I thought they were some kind of Russian ant. It seemed incredible how a Russian peasant could find any kind of rest in such a bed.

We now were closer to the fighting front and saw many dead Russian soldiers awaiting burial. They looked like Orientals, almost Chinese.

Russian Poland had not yet emerged from feudalism. We suddenly would come across a huge, magnificent, castle-like building belonging to a member of the Polish aristocracy, and whenever we could manage it, we would stay there for a little while. Often, some general would be quartered there and we had to protect him. Inside we would see fine oil paintings, huge libraries, Persian carpets, hardwood floors and marvelous stables, while the villagers lived in one-room wooden huts. The only furniture the peasants had consisted of wooden benches going around the room and one table. Usually the floor was made of mud. They cooked in an open fireplace and slept on straw. Very small children were kept in a cradle hanging from the ceiling and were rocked by pulling a string. All land and crops belonged to the man in the castle who seemed to keep these his farmers in complete misery.

Our relations with these illiterate Polish people always were friendly. Nobody could speak Polish or Russian so we communicated by sign language. Communication with the outside world did not exist for them. They had never seen a newspaper. In winter they would be snowed in for several months. They were stoical, friendly and did not seem to care much what happened. The fields, crops, cattle and houses did not belong to them anyway.

In one of the houses I found a samovar which the owner was quite willing to sell. I wanted a receipt to prove I had not stolen it, but I soon found out nobody in the house could write his name. A village leader finally appeared and signed, though it took quite a while. Never before had I contacted such dull people. I saw no stores of any kind where they could buy necessities.

During our weeks of marching around Poland we crossed a single railroad track only once.

The end of October brought bad weather and we felt it would be hard to spend a Russian winter in our little huts. By now, the big offensive had petered out. Large territories had been occupied and more than 100,000 prisoners taken, but the Russian armies had not been encircled and wiped out. The Russians would be unable to undertake an offensive for some time, but Germany could not yet transfer enough divisions from the Eastern Front to knock France and England out of the war. We had the inner lines, but our western enemies controlled the seas which enabled them to import whatever they needed. We remained blockaded and completely sealed off from the rest of the world. I could see no end to this war.

German anti-aircraft batteries still were found ineffective. To correct this situation an anti-aircraft artillery school for officers had been established at Ostende in Belgium. At the beginning of November our lieutenant was ordered to Ostende for a two-week course and during his absence I was in command.

Late that month, during a snowstorm, we were ordered to take position near Duschky to protect huge amounts of all kinds of war materiel arriving every day by train. We were now some 150 miles inside Poland and were told we probably would remain in Duschky for a long time. From the Duschky depot we could obtain everything we needed to construct our own quarters — plenty of lumber, nails, stoves, equipment for electric lights and good roofing. Our men attacked this housing problem with enthusiasm and in a few days we had a warm, solid little house of our own. The lieutenant and I had our own rooms, including the frame of a bed — four posts connected by wires strung crisscross for a sleeping bag. In the other, larger room the men erected comfortable bunks. Everybody was content and happy.

Our guns were in the front yard. In good flying weather we had to be outside. It was very boring, but everybody knew that we led a life comfortable in the extreme, considering a bloody war was going on day and night.

On November 23 the doctor from the 346th Infantry Regiment declared I had jaundice. My face looked yellow and I felt weak. This doctor wanted me to go to a hospital, but I didn't want to and invented all kinds of reasons why I could not possibly leave. Once in a hospital they might have shipped me to Germany and I might not have been allowed to return to the battery. The doctor gave me medicine for an enlarged gallbladder and told me not to eat fat. After two weeks I was much better.

After our lieutenant returned from Flak school our shooting seemed improved. Once in a while we got phone calls from neighboring outfits, telling us we almost shot that last plane down. The Russians received many planes from their allies, especially ones of French make. In good weather we had to be on our toes. We were supposed to protect thousands of tons of valuable war materiel, including many carloads of ammunition, and we thought all this stuff one day would induce the Russians to make a determined attack. One or two bombs dropped at the right place could blow up most of the materiel. But no attack was ever made.

At the end of the year I spent a short leave at home and arrived back in Duschky in the middle of January 1916.

Lt. d. Res. Karl Schroeder, commanding B.A.K. 54.

Kanonier Bruehn of B.A.K. 54 with a Goertz rangefinder in Poland, April 1915.

A French 75 mm. gun rebored to 77 mm., belonging to B.A.K. 54. This scene was repeated often in September 1915 when heavy rains fell in Poland.

Nagel (standing center) and battery mates in front of a dugout in Poland.

NCO mess, Poland. Nagel is seated second from right.

Nagel in front of dugout on Hill 154, Poland.

Nagel, Duschky, Poland, winter 1915.

Offizierstellvertreter Nagel, September 1915.

FOUR

1916

Marking time on the Eastern Front

During 1916 the war became more ferocious every day, on the ground and in the air.

On the Western Front the Allies mounted attacks that resulted in the bloodiest and most costly battles of the war. They attacked with a great superiority of men and materiel on the Somme, while Germany mounted an offensive at Verdun. These were battles of annihilation pure and simple; whichever side suffered the greatest losses was the loser. Infantry divisions consisting of roughly 20,000 men would fight in sectors only 2,000 to 3,000 yards wide. Enormous losses and overall fatigue forced their withdrawal within two or three days. Human beings just could not stand that type of fighting any longer. Artillery was massed wheel to wheel on both sides, and drumfire lasting up to two weeks without interruption was the usual preparation for a new attack. Our infantry was forced to dig deep dugouts to survive and quite often they did not have enough time to climb the ladders leading to the trenches during an enemy attack. Our losses in these battles of attrition became very serious. The Allies thought our armies would collapse under heavy pressure on two fronts, especially since Russia had promised to mount heavy attacks soon.

On the Eastern Front Romania joined our enemies. Situated at the southern end of this front, combined Russian and Romanian armies theoretically, and perhaps with relative ease, could outflank our right wing and roll up the Eastern Front with one big push. To overcome this danger, a newly formed German army attacked and quickly conquered all of Romania in one of the most brilliant campaigns of the war.

By this time both sides had made incredible progress in the air. In 1914 and part of 1915, a soldier might see single planes several times a day in good flying weather. But by 1916 the sight of a formation of 20 or 30 planes was nothing unusual.

To help the infantry, the so-called infantry battle flier came into being. At first, these planes were used for reconnaissance only. During the battles on the Somme it was frequently impossible for a commanding general to know where the front line was. Infantry fliers would fly very low and report their findings by wireless. Naturally, they encountered heavy and effective ground fire, against which they were protected by steel plates later on. But this armor made the planes too slow. Then, a new two-seater battle flier was built with a stronger engine and no armor at all. These planes had two machine-guns, bombs and often hand grenades. Both sides employed this type of plane very extensively and effectively. Thus, a great cry for more and better anti-aircraft artillery arose. The demand for more weapons of all kinds mounted to astronomical figures.

When I returned to the Eastern Front in mid-January, the weather was bad. Snow storms were frequent and we had lots of time on our hands. For days on end snow would fall and every day the crew would go to work with shovels to dig out the guns and keep them ready.

I knew the war would not be over soon, but I never lost sight of my plans to go to the United States. In school all German boys acquired a solid foundation of the English language, but I thought this would be a good time to get acquainted with business language and methods as practiced in England or America. I sent to Germany for all kinds of books and during my idle time in Russia I wrote many business letters, translating from German to English. One book had the correct translation and I finally became reasonably proficient. I also read English books to increase my vocabulary.

By now we had a gramophone which played all day. Needles for it were hard to obtain, until one man found a big box of Russian needles in Wilna.

On March 12 headquarters ordered us to shoot down a Russian balloon which had torn loose. We never saw it. At the same time the headquarters staff informed us a Russian attack was expected and ordered us to keep the horses nearby in case we had to pull out. Nobody seemed to take this threat seriously. The attack did take place and we could hear clearly the rumble and roar of distant fighting. It must have been a large attack because the army newspaper reported our side buried 9,280 Russian soldiers.

Fleas and lice were quite bothersome and I thought it best to have my uniform deloused again. It helped, but after the steaming the uniform looked terrible. We had no pressing facilities.

A 'vacation' in Belgium

On March 27 I was promoted to lieutenant and ordered to proceed immediately to the Flak artillery school at Ostende. I was very happy about this assignment. Life in these officer training schools was always very agreeable and easy, and one always could manage to spend á day or two at home on the way coming or going.

Ostende, a well known Belgian resort city, was only seven miles from the front lines in Flanders. The battlefield of Ypres was just 12 miles to the southwest. Officers attending the school were quartered in the elegant beach hotels. At that time the British army had to fight a severe shortage of ammunition and had given up shelling Ostende, but, we were told, British destroyers sometimes would use the hotels for target practice. We were careful not to show lights in our rooms at night. The rumble of heavy artillery fire from the fighting at Ypres never let up day and night. For a man coming from the Eastern Front, it sounded alarming.

Instructions in the newest fire technique were held in a classroom in Ostende, and the newest rangefinders, speed indicators and tabulations were explained. Theoretically, it should have been possible to shoot down any plane, provided it kept on flying in the same direction, at the same height and speed, and provided the officer commanding the battery was able to quickly transform the data shouted to him by the men manning the various instruments into the right commands. All would have been in vain if the plane changed direction during the six or seven seconds the shrapnel was in flight. Luck remained the most important ingredient for success in this anti-aircraft business.

In the morning lessons we would fire with light cannons at a screen. In good flying weather a bus would take us to the nearby front where the school maintained a battery for training purposes. This battery was stationed 2½ kilometers from Dixmude in Flanders, a location where the fighting never stopped. The name Dixmude was known to every German civilian because it was so often mentioned in the daily war reports.

I was astonished to see the battery in a position which looked like a permanent one: high earthworks around each gun and concrete dugouts for the crews with concrete dining room facilities. One or two heavy shells could wipe out all of this quickly, but the battery obviously was unable to change position in a hurry. It was explained the British knew quite well of the existence and purpose of the battery, but they preferred to keep it in operation to find out whether we had developed new anti-aircraft firing techniques. That close to the front it would have been easy to shoot us up, but knowing the battery would be re-mounted somewhere else the British found it to their advantage to leave us alone. However, they used this battery quite extensively as a training target for their new bomber crews, and in this way both sides found good practice targets. It was peculiar, but as far as I know, up to March 1916 this battery had not shot down a single plane, nor had the British bombing attacks wounded anybody, despite dropping hundreds of bombs. This situation has always puzzled me.

During the time I was here a plane would almost always be in range. Some were observation planes. They were slow and tried to keep out of range, but the most interesting were the British bombers on their training missions. They would come over, an officer trainee would open fire, the bomber would drop a bomb and then the instructor would try to explain what probably went wrong. When it was my turn to direct the firing the bomber came straight at us, rather low. We opened up and from the ground it looked as if we were shooting pretty good. Then I clearly saw the bomb coming down in a big arch, but it obviously would miss us. When it exploded, everybody ducked behind a heavy wall of earth and nothing happened. I thought this bomb might be the only one aimed at me personally, so I ran over to the crater and picked up some vicious and still hot splinters as souvenirs. I had them mounted with the date, April 6, 1916. Coming from the peaceful Eastern Front, these goings-on certainly represented quite a change. But nobody seemed concerned and all had a good time. It was interesting and amusing, like the target shooting of a friendly gun club.

A short distance from the gun positions we were fed fine meals in a sort of dugout dining room. These were leisurely meals with wine, coffee and desserts. We were fully protected on all sides because the dining room was dug in. But the roof, flush with the ground, was only tin and one chance hit would have been too bad. Lingering over coffee with only a tin roof for protection made me uneasy. After all, this was one of the most active battlefields on the Western Front, and some explosions seemed uncomfortably near. Later on, after some high-ranking Air Service officer had to eat there, the roof was reinforced with heavy logs and plenty of earth. While eating, the few windows in the building would never cease rattling.

During the next few days the weather was bad and we had a chance to visit the mole of Zeebrugge, which later became famous as the target of a large scale raid by the British navy. A four-gun battery manned by German navy personnel was stationed at the end of the mole, which I estimated at a half-mile long, going out to sea in a gentle curve. The mole protected a canal going to Bruege where our submarines that operated against England were stationed. For the previous two years the life of this battery had been a peaceful one. It looked to me as if the battery crew consisted of older seamen, too old for combat duty. They were very friendly, showed us around and certainly did not dream they would all be dead soon.

From Ostende to Zeebrugge was only seven miles or so — one continuous beach lined with hotels. A friend of mine lived in one of these hotels, and was attending Flak school when the famous British raid occurred the night of April 22, 1918. According to him, an enormous racket started while he was reading in his hotel room. Somebody banged on his door, shouting something about a British landing. Together with hundreds of other soldiers and officers he grabbed a rifle and ran toward the noise while shells coming from the sea seemed to explode everywhere. It looked to him like a big affair and he wondered whether this might be a large scale, and perhaps very dangerous, landing.

The main trouble was the heavy fog. Except for the crew manning the battery on the mole, nobody seemed to know for sure what was going on.

A few destroyers and two light cruisers came out of the fog. In minutes their point-blank fire had silenced our battery, shooting the men down as they came running from their barracks on the mole to man the guns. Then, British marines, all volunteers, jumped from the destroyers directly onto the mole, finishing off the rest of the battery crew with rifle fire and hand grenades. The two cruisers were filled with cement and did not take part in the fight. They were sunk in the channel with the hope of bottling up our submarines stationed in Bruege.

It was a brilliantly executed raid which almost succeeded. The two cruisers did not quite block the channel and our submarines still could get in and out. However, this raid caused substantial damage and casualties. At first we had no artillery available besides the guns on the mole and the defenders felt helpless while shooting their rifles at the destroyers. There were a few motorized Flak guns in the neighborhood and when they appeared on the scene, raking the mole with point-blank fire, it was felt the enemy would be unable to break out of the mole until reinforcements arrived. At this time it was still foggy and our side did not yet understand the purpose of the raid. The whole fight was over in an hour or so, and only when the fog lifted and the British had left could one clearly see the damage and the raid's intent. After the war I read that several British soldiers had received the Victoria Cross. *

On the German side, the generals began to understand that motorized K Flak could do more than just shoot at planes.

Trench life in Latvia

On April 16 I arrived back on the Eastern Front. Our quarters were as comfortable as ever, but we noticed a difference in our food supply. Up to now there seemed to be ample food — plenty of meat, fat, even butter — and while most food in Germany was rationed we still were amply supplied. But now we received only so many grams of this or that, along with instructions not to be wasteful. According to the newspapers, food would be scarce until huge harvests from the occupied territories came in. But in reality, food became scarcer until, by the end of the war, soldiers and civilians alike were severely undernourished and weakened by the successful total blockade of Germany.

Compared with the Western Front, activity in the air was very mild.

---

* The raid at Zeebrugge occurred the night of April 22-23 (St. George's Day), 1918. Of the some 500 Royal Marines and British seamen who attacked the mole from the deck of HMS Vindictive that night, 11 were awarded the Victoria Cross. On the German side, **Hauptmann** Schuette, commander of the batteries on the mole, received the Knight's Cross of the Royal Order of Hohenzollern with Swords. — R.A.B.

On April 25 a Russian flier tried to bomb a neighboring Flak battery. Six bombs were dropped. All missed. In our peaceful war this was something to talk about for days.

To kill time, everybody wrote long letters home. On May 4, for instance, I wrote four letters to friends of mine in the army, hoping to get replies someday.

On July 18 an officer of the General Staff appeared and declared that our efforts toward winning the war amounted to absolutely nothing. We agreed, but don't blame us. We were here because somebody told us to be here. If necessary, our battery would be shipped to another sector to be used as field artillery. The best field artillery had been sent to the Western Front where it was badly needed. Our artillery line here was very thin and every gun had to be made available to repulse Russian attacks which were expected soon. It seemed our holiday was about over.

At the end of July we were loaded on flatcars and shipped north to the front in Latvia, with instructions to report to the commander of the 4th Cavalry Division stationed near Dunaburg. The general, one of the sons of the Grand Duke of Mecklenburg, was extremely polite and after welcoming us, he invited the commander and I to a fine dinner. He gave us a picture of the overall situation and what he expected us to do.

Our lines were very thinly held. We had very little artillery and the front line trenches were manned by dismounted cavalry. The general did not admit what everybody knew: namely, that these men were vastly inferior to our regular infantry. For months they had been on this quiet front, lacked training and experience and no one could be sure what would happen if there was a serious Russian attack.

We took position some 700 yards behind the trenches. The next day a captain of the dragoons took me to the front line to introduce me to his company commanders, and to let me have a look at the Russian lines. I was astonished to see the Duna River, about 200 yards wide, between us and the Russians. Our front line trenches looked solid. A rifleman could be seen looking toward the enemy every 10 yards or so and in front of us, down to the river's edge, were endless rolls of barbed wire, entangled to form a solid mass of obstacles. I could not believe how any troops could penetrate this heavy maze of wire in the face of rifle fire. But apparently I was quite wrong. In bad weather Russian troops came over in small boats during the night, silently cutting a path through the wire and successfully raided our trenches. No shots were fired, but the sentry would be quietly stabbed. The Russians even succeeded in penetrating to the dugouts where they would cut everyone's throats before a nearby sentry could notice what had happened. We just did not have enough men to properly man these trenches. The general felt a Russian attack might succeed easily if they could concentrate enough heavy artillery to pulverize the barbed wire, and then come over quickly on rafts and boats in great numbers. Their superiority in men and guns was estimated at 10 to one. After listening to these reports I felt the real war had caught up with me again. We were told to zero in on various targets so we could hit boats and troops while embarking on their way across.

The next day we established phone connections between the battery and an observation post from which I was supposed to direct our fire in case of trouble. On the other end of this line our lieutenant would make the necessary corrections or change targets by following my observations telephoned to him from my O.P.

The post was built solidly and I felt only a direct hit from above would be fatal. I could look toward the Russian trenches through a tripod, rabbit ear-type binocular and did not have to expose my head while observing. Rifle fire came over sporadically, just enough to force everybody to keep their heads down. To the right of us was the village of Swonki. We were told to zero in on Swonki because it surely would be used as a troop concentration point in case of a planned attack. It was not difficult to obtain all the data we needed to cover targets within 5,000 yards of us, but we could not collect this data without firing a few registering shots at each target. The company commanders did not like that. In their opinion we would provoke the Russians to fire at our nice trenches in retaliation.

Shortly thereafter, more Russian observation planes than usual flew over — mostly Farmans and Nieuports. On some days we were quite busy. Even Russian heavy caliber shells, making an eerie sounding noise, came over our heads and we wondered what they were shooting at.

Our commanding lieutenant was called to the sector's artillery commander, who told him a heavy attack was expected. The High Command was uneasy because our lines were very thin and we had little artillery and only a small reserve. Our fliers also had detected preparations for a gas attack. We were ordered to surround our position with barbed wire and to bring the horses to safety further back. Retreat was forbidden. All gas masks and gas alert systems had to be checked. I was ordered to appear with one NCO and three men for training in hand grenade throwing. We survived this lesson, but to hold such a sizzling bomb in hand and then count to seven before throwing was an uncomfortable experience.

I had to spend the next few days in my rather uncomfortable observation post. I could doze, but there was not room enough to stretch out. An attack probably would be launched just before dawn, but the whole thing looked very improbable to me. Our sentries were doubled, everybody slept with their clothes on and at the critical times before dawn, the Russian lines constantly were illuminated by Very lights. I was in contact with the lieutenants commanding the companies, and none of them took the situation seriously. We all thought these alerts and preparations were pretty silly. All of us had peered over at the Russians for hours without noticing anything unusual. Finally the alert petered out and I went back to my comfortable bed in our dugout.

On September 9 I was decorated with the Iron Cross second class for no special reason at all. It was the general opinion that every officer and many of the men would get the decoration unless they were found running away and refused to stop until they reached home. It had no value and neither had the Cross of the Hanseatic League, which I received a short time later.

The German army did not give medals unless they were earned. Too many Iron Crosses second class had been given out, even to officers and men who fought the war at some nice, clean desk. The Iron Cross first class was much harder to obtain. For ordinary soldiers or non-commissioned officers it was the highest decoration obtainable. The Pour le Merite was the highest decoration, reserved for officers. It rarely was given. Most were in the hands of fighter pilots and submarine commanders, but some commanders of ground troops earned it, too. As with the other decorations, the lower the rank the more difficult it was to earn. In addition to these medals, an officer or outfit fighting with distinction could be mentioned in dispatches. Usually a congratulatory message from the commanding general would follow and this was considered the first step toward earning a Pour le Merite. The British would give the Victoria Cross, or the Americans would give the Medal of Honor to combat soldiers for one outstanding deed, but to earn the Pour le Merite, as a rule, you had to prove sustained courage in several hair-raising exploits. The only exception I know of was General Ludendorff. *

On October 27, at 10:50 a.m., the Russians suddenly hit us with a salvo of five shots of 75 mm. shrapnel. It was a good sunny day and while we were standing around looking at the sky, we heard them coming and had time enough to jump into the slit trenches built for that purpose. Nobody was hurt, but we wondered if they intended to shoot us out of our comfortable quarters. We waited and waited, but nothing happened and we concluded these must have been some stray shots. However, every window in our rather luxurious quarters was broken.

A short time later we had a visit from a neighboring Flak battery. Its officer, who had just come back from the Flak school in Ostende, reported the friendly understanding with the British there had come to an end. It seemed the British became sufficiently annoyed with the training battery, and one fine day very heavy caliber salvos smashed the

---

* Nagel's statement concerning medals is evidenced by the number of men who received the **Eisernes Kreuz II. Klasse** (Iron Cross second class) in just one German regiment alone during the First World War. For example, from mid-May 1915 to the end of June 1917, no less than 1,862 officers and men from **Infanterie-Regiment Nr. 161 (10. Rheinisches)** received the decoration. This contrasts with only one bestowal of the **Orden Pour le Merite** to a member of the same regiment, and that to the lieutenant colonel commanding.

The mention of General Erich von Ludendorff refers to his actions on August 6-7, 1914, when he took command of a lost brigade in the German assault on Liege, Belgium, and captured the citadel there. For this single incident Ludendorff received the **Orden Pour le Merite**. — R.A.B.

four guns, the mess hall and everything else to bits. A new battery had been set up out of artillery range.

At the beginning of November the cavalry wanted me to spend a few days with them in my old observation post because the Russians seemed to be up to something. Every night our outposts could hear them working and digging. I clearly could hear them myself, shouting and laughing. They must have been working on railroad tracks because every night we could hear the puffing and clatter of a slow-moving train. The general wanted us to hit the train and stop the Russians from working.

I had to direct the shooting by ear only. In these cold Russian winter nights any kind of noise carried a long way. I could hear the train coming and some nights it sounded like a real battle. One or two 77 mm. shells might not stop a train so whenever I thought it time to fire, we let go with a barrage of 20 or more shots, hoping for the best. This train shoot developed into a kind of sport. It was quite impressive and our cavalry friends looked forward to the nightly fun, but nobody knew whether we hit the target. For a time the train would cease running, but we could not stop the traffic entirely.

The division was commanded by a cavalry general who thought this comfortable trench life had made his officers fat, lazy and unfit. So, out of the blue sky, he ordered a fox hunt to be held on the first decent day. All officers not on duty had to participate. We knew we had no foxes or hounds, but the general, no doubt, would arrange to have plenty of obstacles for us to jump over on a several-mile course.

Our outfit was ordered to send one officer. The lieutenant was 46 or 47 years old and for more than 20 years before the war had not been on a horse. His horse, "Adolph," was the best we had. Since crossing the Polish border, Adolph had never gone faster than a very slow trot on rare occasions. So far he had walked across Poland. But he was the only horse in our outfit that sometimes would prance a little when feeling frisky.

The lieutenant flatly refused to go. He was on the fat side, not at all interested in riding as a sport and was unwilling to risk his neck to amuse the general. Of course, I had to go. I never had ridden Adolph and there was no time for lengthy tryouts or training. I jumped him a few times over some broomsticks and thought he could at least see the obstacles.

The chase took place on a beautiful November day. It was explained we had to follow the leader over all hurdles for about three kilometers. The hurdles were narrow and I wondered what would happen if 100 riders arrived at the hurdles at the same time. But a few minutes after the start the field thinned out and Adolph amazed me. In private life he must have been a racehorse and a good one. He would not tolerate another horse in front of him and jumped the hurdles with the greatest of ease. All I had to do was gently lift his head before jumping and hold him while landing. It was quite a ride.

The first few hurdles were not difficult, but in the middle of the course we had to jump three in a row, one after the other, only a few yards apart. Adolph seemed to enjoy it, but I lost my left stirrup and was in the process of falling off when the rider next to me grabbed me by the belt and held it until my foot found the stirrup. I was grateful to that fellow because it could have been a nasty fall. We were among the leading riders and some 80 horses came up thundering behind us. We ended that ride in a blaze of glory and when I came back nobody would believe that Adolph was as good a horse as could be found in the cavalry division. I was afraid some ranking officer might find a way to take him away from us.

At the end of November the Russians fired a few shots into our lines every day without aiming at anything in particular. We were ordered to retaliate, hoping they would stop their senseless shooting. On November 28, 20 shots landed around our battery without doing any damage.

For the first time we heard of some peace overtures started by the German government, but nothing came of it. Our government talked as if we were the victors, while the Allies now believed firmly they would have us on the ropes before long. Some very sharp notes had been exchanged with the U.S. government and we still were arguing about the American lives lost on the Lusitania the year before. The entrance of the United States into the war on the side of the Allies was very probable. Germany was suffering from all kinds of shortages and this German peace offensive was considered a first sign of cracking up.

For Christmas we had a nice tree and plenty of beer.

Sporting sunglasses, Schroeder and Nagel catch up on the latest news.

German observation balloon. (Photo courtesy of Paul M. Smith).

Nagel (left) and an officer friend 'show off' newly introduced steel helmets in a posed photograph for Nagel's family back in Germany.

Fritz and Dorothy.

FIVE

1917

Final days in the east

In January the snow was very deep in Russia, making it impossible to walk even short distances. Snowshoes were issued.

I again was ordered to attend the Flak school in Ostende from February 1st to the 18th. It was the same routine and I did not understand why they sent me there again, although I was very glad to go. No new firing techniques had been developed, but I had another nice vacation and I visited my family for a couple of days.

On my return to the battery on February 24, excitement prevailed because a few days before the Russians had made a successful raid on our lines. They penetrated to the farmhouse where the general slept, silently killed all the sentries and abducted the general. At this time the Duna River was frozen solid and in a snowstorm it was impossible to prevent raiders from getting through. Headquarters now wanted the sentries checked more often by officers and I was ordered to help the undermanned cavalry by patrolling and checking their sentries several times a week, always at night.

To walk on snowshoes for half an hour was strenuous. For protection against the terrible cold I had to wear very heavy clothes, heavy boots and a sweater-like cover for the head and face. All this gear made walking on snowshoes difficult and very slow. Once in a while some bullets would zing by, probably aimed at nothing in particular, and hit nearby branches which would fall with a crack that could be heard for some distance. Most of my way went through a forest until I reached the approach trench. I did not like this job at all and what worried me was the fact that even a slight wound might prevent me from walking and would mean certain death by freezing. Nobody would miss me for a few hours. To sit down and rest was dangerous. I was told to shoot my Very light pistol if I should meet a Russian raiding party. I never saw a Russian. But I was glad when the Duna finally began to melt, making raids more unlikely.

It seemed the Russian army was incapable of mounting serious attacks and some of our units were shipped to the Western Front where reinforcements were needed badly.

On March 13 a Farman doubledecker came into range while I was on duty. We were shooting pretty well, but not better than usual, when all of a sudden the plane came down, burning and breaking up in three parts. The army High Command gave me official recognition after hearing witnesses. It took two witnesses before a kill could be certified officially. The flier, a Captain Rasowski, was saved although wounded. While in the hospital he stated that our fire did not bother him at all. According to him, a German fighter had shot him down. But there were no fighters in the air at that time. *

At the end of March, revolution broke out in Russia and we wondered what would happen next. No doubt we would be shipped to the Western Front sooner or later, where the situation was touch and go. The Allies wanted to break through to final victory while Russia was still in the fight.

Division headquarters wanted me to attend an officers' gas school in Berlin starting May 14 and lasting 10 days. Of course, I was delighted. The Russians were reported to have plenty of gas which they might release at once in desperation. So far, no big gas attacks had occurred, but division headquarters wanted one officer trained in the newest techniques of gas defense. I could not understand why they picked me for this job. Somebody with technical training certainly would have been better.

Arriving in Berlin we were well quartered in a hotel, but it quickly became evident that food was very scarce. We had to feed ourselves in restaurants and were given food cards — so many ounces of this and that. No restaurant would serve us without surrendering these coupons first. To obtain a satisfying meal was quite impossible; even potatoes were scarce. The rations of meat, butter or sugar were just enough to whet one's appetite for more. The bread looked very dark and the flour reputedly was mixed with wood shavings. It was no pleasure eating and everybody was always hungry.

About 400 officers attended this gas warfare school every 10 days. We

---

* According to the German Air Service publication, **"Der Nachrichtenblatt der deutschen Luftstreitkräfte,"** this Farman was credited to Nagel as his first official victory. Possibly a Farman F.30, a type used mostly in Russia from 1916 on, the plane crashed into barbed wire entanglements in front of the German front lines not far from Dunaburg. At the time, Nagel was deputy commander of **Flakzug 66**, a unit he was transferred to after having served 26 months with **B.A.K. 54**. Although his narrative neglects to mention this transfer which occurred on March 6, 1917, his 1917 diary states he was associated with **Flakzug 66** until October of that year. This unit's commanding officer was a **Leutnant** Kunath.

In subsequent correspondence concerning this oversight in his narrative, Nagel explained: "The rule was that one officer must always be with the battery. Because well trained Flak officers were scarce, many of us were shifted around a good deal to fill a vacancy. Life in each battery was more or less the same, and nobody paid any attention to the number on the shoulder boards. All in all, life with **Flak 66** was most comfortable and boring." — R.A.B.

were told what type of weather was needed for a successful gas attack, how our warning system had to be set up and how to take care of the equipment. To prove the effectiveness of our latest gas mask model, we were led into a room containing a lethal dose of phosgene gas. We remained inside a few minutes without ill effect. The course ended with a field exercise showing how a gas attack should be mounted. In order not to contaminate our uniforms, overalls were issued and we had to walk through the cloud coming toward us. My gas mask seemed to fit perfectly. I could not smell anything. The colonel giving the instructions seemed obsessed with the cost of killing an enemy. According to him, gas warfare was the most effective and cheapest of all weapons. He was a fanatic on the subject and had statistics to prove his point.

Upon my return to the Eastern Front everybody seemed certain the Russians would collapse soon.

On June 12 I received orders to proceed to Ghent, Belgium, for a two-week course in optical instruments. I suddenly was elected to be the division's optical officer, but I had no idea what my duties would be.

I was gradually becoming the envy of my comrades. Most officers attended, perhaps, one special training course, but many never had a chance to get away from their front line duties at all, except when they obtained home leaves. This was my third special assignment to another plush course, far away from the fighting. I was asked how I managed to obtain all these special favors. I was astonished myself and did not know why. I had to admit there was some favoritism going on, although I had no idea who was responsible. To give me a few weeks in Berlin to train in gas warfare, and then completely ignore that training and appoint me optical officer, which again required more schooling, looked suspicious. Or, at least, it could not readily be explained.

Arriving in Ghent on June 16, I found the weather quite hot. My heat rash bothered me and the doctor gave me some salve which did no good. One of the troubles was my uniform was quite dirty, but there was no chance of having it cleaned while traveling so much. From June 18 to July 5 we were lectured on the newest developments in optics and how to repair and maintain the instruments. In private life the lecturing officer was an engineer at the famous Zeiss Works in Leipzig. But his elaborate formulas had no practical value for me. The only worthwhile suggestions we learned were the following: To train a man as a range finder he had to be above average in intelligence and he had to be able to give the correct range within 10 seconds. Men who were nervous, more than 40 years old, wore glasses or had bad feet were not suitable.

After this lecture course was over — it was the first of its kind — we were asked to give our opinions in writing. Ten percent of the participants claimed to be pleased. Ninety percent thought the course useless. Whatever practical benefits we derived from it could have been taught easily in a few hours. None of us had enough school training to re-

motely understand the complicated optical formulas. But a good time
was had by all and nobody was anxious to return to the front.

During the summer of 1917, the revolution in Russia had undermined
the discipline of the Czar's armies and our High Command was most
anxious to terminate the war on the Eastern Front. The negotiations
with Trotzky and Lenin dragged on for months. The Russians were unwilling to surrender unconditionally. For a time, the Kerensky government came to power and we were told further heavy fighting might be
the prospect.

Russian battle plans had been found on a Russian officer and according to these plans, one more do-or-die attack seemed certain. On paper
the Russian superiority looked frightening. Our division, consisting of
rifle-carrying cavalry — by no means a first class fighting outfit — was
to be attacked by several Russian divisions, with one cavalry division
in reserve for mopping up. According to the plan, of which I had a copy,
the position of our guns would be overrun during the first day of the attack. But nobody thought the situation would ever be serious.

To our surprise the attack started in the morning and the Russians
evidently were not short of artillery or ammunition. Some heavy shells
made it uncomfortable for us, but we received no hits. We clearly could
see their shells exploding in our infantry positions and it looked like a
very heavy fight. But by noon the Russians had not even been able to
enter our forward trenches, which we were willing to give up should
the pressure become too great. The division lost 275 dead and more
than 300 wounded. Our services to act as field artillery were not needed
and the fighting soon died out.

During this battle we were puzzled when we saw some 20 or 30 Russian soldiers coming in formation toward our guns in the early afternoon. They marched in rows of four or five, their rifles over their
shoulders. At first we thought they were our soldiers, but soon their
long bayonets and typically Russian hats made it clear, to our surprise,
who they were. Obviously they had no intentions of fighting us, but simply seemed to be going to our rear. We stared at them when they
passed. Nobody did anything and soon they disappeared.

The year 1917 was one of ferocious Allied attacks on the Western
Front. This front had to be held until the 80 German divisions in Russia
could be added to our forces in the west for one final victorious blow. In
fact, for the first time in this war, we would have had a slight numer-
ical superiority, provided we could mount a final attack before substantial aid could come from the United States, which had entered the
fight against us in April.

Our enemies recognized this danger and were most anxious to knock
us out before we could make the shift. The terrible battles of Verdun,
the Somme, Arras and Flanders were the result. Our losses with

names, ranks and dates of death appeared daily in the newspapers, but these endless lists were now thicker than the paper. It was quite frightening to the German people. Thousands of names every day, divided into infantry, cavalry, artillery, air force and service troops. The navy published its own lists.

The German people never quite understood why the United States joined forces with the Allies. American lives were lost on the Lusitania, but why did American citizens travel on a British steamer carrying all kinds of war material? Much was said concerning the freedom of the seas, guaranteed by all seafaring nations, but the British navy stopped all neutrals from shipping food to Germany.

American banks had financed ammunition purchases for the British and French armies and in case of a French-British collapse, billions of dollars would never be paid. From an economics standpoint, an Allied victory was a necessity. Against these powerful pressures, Germany was helpless. German propaganda in America was clumsy, while British views prevailed in most American newspapers.

In April 1917 the U.S. Congress declared war, but the German people were not too frightened. We knew the Americans had a small army and navy and we could not see how these forces could influence the war's events. It would take years for them to mobilize and by that time the war would be over. The average German knew very little about American history, and while thinking about American soldiers, he visualized an army of cowboys appearing on the battlefield with their funny hats and lassos, like Teddy Roosevelt and his Rough Riders. Surely they would not amount to much on the Western Front. But some educated people, especially those in north Germany who knew the United States well, now feared it might be impossible to win. The Americans were fresh; for them the war had just started while we were exhausted after three long years of fighting. And no one knew for sure what the Americans would accomplish now that the chips were down.

For the Allies, America's entry into the fight completely changed their plans. Victory was assured. All they had to do was hold out until newly formed American armies could be thrown into the battle against the German foe. Without American help the war would have ended through mutual exhaustion without victory.

By the summer of 1917 our food rations were reduced again. Bread without fat and marmalade made from turnips were our main foods. There was hardly any meat in our daily menu of vegetable soup. I was always hungry.

Wartime nuptials

On October 22 I left the Eastern Front for good, although I did not know it then. The group commander had obtained a four-week leave for me to get married. When the train reached Wilna in Poland, I was paged by a messenger and handed a telegram stating my leave had been cancelled. I was to proceed immediately to the Western Front and join the heavy motorized Flak battery Nr. 179. Of course, this caused consternation, but I was determined to marry first and then proceed to my new destination. I could not see why a few days could make much difference, especially since this heavy battery seemed to be a new weapon requiring a few weeks of special training. On October 24 I arrived in Bremen and the next day my fiancee, Dorothy, and I were married before the proper authorities. On the 26th we were married a second time in my parent's home by the pastor of St. Rembert's Church. We would have preferred a church wedding, but there was no coal available to heat the large church. All my friends were in the army and the only guests were relatives and my family. My godfather was the largest florist in Bremen and had erected a pretty altar in our house. As was the custom, I was married in uniform.

On our honeymoon we spent one day in Hamburg and a day in Berlin, where we visited Dorothy's brother who had been interned as a British subject of military age. When the war broke out he happened to be in Bremen for a week's visit. He had worked for Lever Brothers in London. At the time he was sick and we visited him in a sanitarium belonging to or operated by a prisoner camp. These civilian Englishmen received food parcels from England in great quantities and we found plenty of meat, chocolate, butter, biscuits, coffee, tea and many more fine things which we had not tasted for months. Although I wore a uniform, the atmosphere was quite friendly and the other prisoners crowded around us. They were short of smokes so we exchanged cigarettes and smoking tobacco for food. When we left that evening our handbag was so heavy with food I could hardly carry it. I would have preferred to have gone into that prison camp in civilian clothes, but in the German army, the wearing of mufti was not allowed. Besides, I had not worn my suits for three years.

Our marriage had not been just a thought of the moment. To marry an enemy alien in wartime created abnormal problems. Is there any law against it? Dorothy had some money in England she inherited from her father on an insurance policy that was due and payable after the outbreak of war. Would that be lost? The American consul in Bremen, Mr. Fee, had been a friend of my mother-in-law for some time and he was most helpful. All British subjects still in Germany were under his protection until the United States entered the war. We were sure no personal troubles would arise after we were married. In fact, life would be easier for Dorothy. For some time, overeager "patriots" had accused her of espionage, anti-German remarks and trying to signal enemy fliers during an alert. Every time such an accusation was made, Dorothy had to appear before the police commissioner who was an educated and friendly man. He did not believe any of these stories were true, but he finally restricted her to the city of Bremen. She was not allowed to go to the country by bicycle, as most people did regularly. Inspite of this order Dorothy visited her friends in the country. Finally, she had to report to the local police station several times a day to prove she was not up to any earthshaking mischief.

The local police were very friendly. Whenever Dorothy was late they would actually phone her, urging her to come at once to avoid trouble. I believe the police commissioner was happy to approve our marriage just to get rid of this absurd spy problem. After our marriage she became a German citizen and was treated as such, and suddenly, nobody seemed to care anymore what she did or where she went. It all seemed very illogical to me.

Return to the Western Front

I left Bremen October 31 and the next day arrived in Valenciennes, where I met the commander of the new heavy Flak battery. First, we had to learn how to drive an automobile. Up to now, motorized Flak had been driven by chauffeurs — men who had operated automobiles before the war as professional chauffeurs, racing drivers or truck drivers. These men were privates or non-coms. But whenever they were not in the mood or were afraid, they would pretend to be sick, or claim the motor needed repairs, thus immobilizing the outfit whenever it pleased them. To overcome this problem, officers had to learn to drive as well. They also had to understand how the motor functioned so they could detect whether the driver was faking.

Driving school lasted almost all of November and it was very pleasant. In those days all cars were open and the gearshift was located outside on the running board. There were 30 officers and two light touring cars for training so everybody could drive a short time every day. It was great fun. Once I asked the instructor to let me drive the bus carrying all of us to a classroom. The streets in Valenciennes were narrow and as I turned a corner, I suddenly saw a deep canal in front of me. I must have panicked and could not remember how to stop. The chauffeur next to me took over, but I had enough. I felt we surely would land in the deep water and drown. When this training course was over, all of us were still very poor drivers. We understood the theory of a motor, but that was all.

After a few days we were told the Krupp Works had not delivered our guns. In the meantime I was ordered to report to Flak battery Nr. 710, which was in position at the front near Le Cateau. This was an ordinary horsedrawn anti-aircraft outfit, similar to the one I was with on the Eastern Front. But this situation was vastly more uncomfortable. The guns were surrounded by a sea of mud. It was very cold and snowy one day and rainy the next. We slept in dugouts that were very deep, cold, clammy and had four exits. For beds we used planks and covered them with straw. The overall situation in this sector was tense and nobody dared undress at night. Life was miserable. I was always hungry, cold and wondered how long I could stand this sort of life without getting sick.

Our dugouts were relatively safe from artillery fire. Only if all four exits caved in would we be in danger of suffocating, but it was said these dugouts were too deep. We could reach the exits only by climbing up the ladder-like steps one man at a time. It happened in other sectors that the enemy would throw hand grenades down the entrances before anybody knew an attack was going on. Constant artillery fire made it difficult to decide if the heavy stuff coming over should be considered the prelude to a real attack. After a few days our senses became dulled to a point where we did not care much what happened next. The only symbol of comfort down in our hole was a candle stuck in a bottle, flickering in the cold draft and illuminating the faces of dirty and forlorn soldiers. Nobody said much.

British artillery constantly kept the whole area under fire. High explosives were mixed with gas shells, forcing us to wear our gas masks for hours. A gas mask was only safe if it fit very tight and this could best be achieved over a well-shaved chin. The steel blades furnished us for shaving were of poor quality, and to keep myself fairly well shaved was quite an ordeal under those circumstances. We had sentries out day and night to give the gas alarm. One whiff of poison gas would either kill or cripple a man for the rest of his life.

Fortunately, we were on flat ground. Gas lingered in gullies and depressions for quite a while. A gas shell exploded with a light, puffy noise, and if the wind was right the gas cloud traveled a hundred yards quickly. To see such a poisonous cloud move toward you was unnerving and I always was afraid my mask might not fit tight enough.

In good flying weather activities in the air were tremendous. Both sides were trying to push their observation planes deep into enemy territory, accompanied by droves of fighter planes. Great air battles took place all over the sky. The machine-guns sounded like childrens' pop guns and from the ground these melees in the air, involving perhaps 75 to 100 planes, looked quite harmless and were very interesting to watch. By the time the noise of the fighting had reached the ground, the first victims began to drop from the sky. The sight of a falling, burning plane was bad enough, but to see a man fall, turning over and over in the air until he crashed, was a terrible sight.

We were told not to fire on enemy planes if our fighter aircraft were near, but on some days we managed to fire 50 to 100 rounds, apparently without hitting anything. On good days bursting shells in the air all over the front were a common sight. We must have had many anti-aircraft batteries in this neighborhood.

Our rest quarters were in Villers-Outreaux, a few miles behind the front. After spending a week or so in the front lines, these rear quarters seemed like heaven. We could wash properly, scrape the mud from our shoes and coats and sit down to something nice and warm to eat. The first night sleeping in a real bed again seemed too good to be true. Our standards of living and comfort in the front lines were about as low as people could endure. Any change for the better in rear quarters made us feel like human beings, but this pleasurable feeling was dampened by the knowledge that in three days we had to live again like frightened rats.

Self-preservation is a strong impulse and usually is engendered by fright, but discipline and military training, plus a feeling of responsibility an officer should have, kept these emotions in balance. It was never easy for me. It was difficult to control these reactions, especially if one was terribly tired, and I was always tired. Lofty feelings of patriotism, love of country and so forth did not play a role. Nobody I knew thought in those terms. Perhaps, after a nice hot bath, a good meal and a clean uniform a man's patriotism may have come to the fore again, but it quickly was washed away in the mud and misery of the trenches. Most men I knew did the best they could, but the better educated had a greater compulsion to force themselves to be good soldiers. Some people are born more or less fearless. I knew fighter pilots who wished the war would go on forever. They had a wonderful time. It certainly would have been much easier for me had I been born fearless. What is now known as battle fatigue was unknown. I heard that many soldiers, especially in the infantry, lost their minds in combat. But until they visibly became crazy, nobody paid any attention to their condition.

There must be a definite limit to the amount of physical and emotional stress a man can take and I wondered how our enemies were taking it.

The newspapers reported that our negotiations with Russia were making progress, but no peace treaty had been signed and important segments of the army remained on the Eastern Front. Our High Command wanted the Russian war settled to move troops to the west and attack before American help became decisive. The German government made all kinds of peace overtures toward our western enemies, which were rejected flatly. They had us on the ropes and knew it.

At the end of December I was sent home for two week's furlough.

A 77 mm. field piece in position for firing at aircraft, Russia, May 1917.

Driving and mechanics school for Flak officers in Lille, November 1917.

A captured Nieuport 17 of the Royal Flying Corps with German markings, June 1917.

Drawing of anti-aircraft rangefinding. Photocopied by Nagel at Flak school, Ghent, June 1917.

Nagel in the uniform worn while with Flakzug 66.

SIX

1918

'The ideal weapon'

On January 5 I returned from leave. After all the comforts of home life, the sight of the battlefield created in me a feeling of almost hopeless resignation. Muddy craters, ruined houses, bare trees, tired soldiers shuffling along with heavy loads of mud caked on their feet, the puffs of gas shells and the peculiar stink of high explosives were accepted as a way of life.

Activity in the air was quite heavy. On most days we fired about 100 shots. On other days, more than 400. So far enemy planes had not attacked us directly, but concentrated on bombing and shooting up our infantry positions.

I was trying hard to be transferred to a light K Flak, which was something quite new. K stood for Kraftwagen, the German word for automobile. A K Flak was a 77 mm. field gun mounted on an open truck so it could be elevated high enough to fire at aircraft. It looked like the ideal weapon to me. Above all it had mobility, enabling the crew to pick its own location and travel wherever it wanted within its sector. And at night the crew was free to find some reasonably safe place to sleep. At least that was the way I pictured it, and I was certain that a change to K Flak would be an improvement over my present existence. I heard these K Flaks were supposed to hit hard. Each had a well-picked, trained crew and would be commanded by "young officers only," according to the latest pamphlet. I was now 25 years old and I worried I might be too old. Because K Flaks were supposed to fight primarily against low flying enemy battle fliers, they were under the command of the Air Service. The K Flak crews also were supposed to be the glamor boys of the artillery and soon aped the dress and manners of the real glamor boys, the fighter pilots. Each K Flak gun had one officer, and he personally would not carry a weapon. He was supposed to dash around the battlefield wearing only a silk officer's cap instead of the heavy steel helmet, besides being well dressed and clean looking. The Air Service had requested 1,500 of these guns. All this was very appealing. To strut around once again in a clean uniform seemed a wonderful way of life to me at the time.

But, while waiting for a better assignment, I had to remain where I was in a position near Belincourt. A small stove was installed in our dugout. It was still too cold to take off our heavy overcoats, but the stove helped.

We were 1,800 yards behind the front line trenches. Right behind us appeared peculiar-looking small guns, described as anti-tank guns. So far I had not seen a tank, although rumors had it our enemies were constructing them in great quantities.

One day I saw a K Flak for the first time. The officer in charge of it explained that he and his crew were driving back to very comfortable quarters every night. All crew members looked clean and happy. I hoped my transfer would come through soon.

On January 10 and 11 heavy shells fell on our position, especially at night. The orders were to have a sentry outside at all times to warn of gas shells or any unusual happenings, but that seemed a silly order under the circumstances. No man could live long standing and watching so I told the soldier to stand on the top step of our dugout where he had a chance to take cover. Only a direct hit in the entrance could kill him.

These nights were quite bad. The earth would shake, sand would drip down on us through the heavy timbers supporting the walls, and we wondered if the whole thing would hold or collapse. The next morning we saw 10 big craters in our position. One gun was knocked over and everybody was sorry the remaining gun was still in operating condition. The approach trench to the guns was flattened and we had to dig another one.

On January 13 we were ordered to change position. Enemy artillery was well zeroed-in on us and staying there invited disaster. To move our two guns with all the ammunition and other gear by hand power alone in that mud was a backbreaking undertaking. As an officer I was not supposed to do manual labor, but I could not help pitching in as I was as anxious as anyone to get away before the enemy thought of us again.

In our new position we immediately started digging a deep dugout and hoped the enemy would not take an interest in us before we had a place to take cover. After a few days it was ready and looked good enough. We even managed to get a load of fresh straw which we placed over some boards, making our sleeping quarters quite comfortable. As I tried to sleep the first night, I clearly could hear underground digging, or rather, drilling. It was unmistakable. The idea of mining and then blowing up one another's position was a type of warfare well known by that time, and by no means rare. I had seen pictures of craters in which field artillery guns as well as front line infantry positions were buried. The British and Germans had mobilized their skilled miners for this new terror and there seemed to be no limit to what they could do.

I reported my apprehension and soon an engineering officer came to listen to my story. He explained the British would have a hard time drilling very far because of the unusually heavy rock formations in the area. He promised to report, but after he was gone I realized his visit could have no practical results as far as we were concerned. Surely they would not pull us out of our position because the enemy might blow us up one day. Maybe they would mass some extra reserves behind us to take our place in case of a big blowup. Whichever way I tried to reason, all we could do was sit and hope. Within a few days this listening to the underground drilling was a pastime for the whole crew. It played on our nerves, but nobody mentioned it directly. I do not know whether an explosion took place later or not, but what saved us from further worry was a report from a technical outfit to our group commander. It overheard a British artillery observation plane telegraphing to a battery, giving it our position and requesting a few salvos for us. We were ordered to change position again and I was happy about it.

Finally, on January 30, I received orders to report to K Flak Nr. 82 in Beaurevoir. Several K Flaks were under the command of a regular army captain who was a very nice fellow. All of the K Flak officers of his command lived in the same large building where they could eat and sleep. I slept in a French bed filled with some sort of feathers with a big linen sheet for a cover. It looked wonderful. From now on it would be strictly a war deluxe for me. I was very happy.

Each morning before dawn the guns would be ready to go and the captain allocated on a map the territory in which each gun was to operate. Our infantry had to be protected from enemy fliers, who now appeared in swarms. That was our job, although we could shoot at any other targets coming into range. We especially were warned to look out for tanks. Serious breakthrough attempts always were spearheaded by tanks.

When we arrived at our sector we found a landscape of complete desolation. The battles of the Somme were fought here. Nothing was left of the little towns. Not one single house was standing, only ruins. Thousands of shell craters filled with water made it difficult for us to proceed. The ruins we were in originally had been the small country towns of La Terriere and Hounecourt. In front of us was a broad, sloping hill also covered with ruins and strongly held by the enemy. Through my binoculars I could see the rim of his trenches, 1,000 yards away.

We were too close to the front lines to remain long in one spot. Mobility was our strong point so we moved every hour, or sooner, if we had fired on fliers more than once or twice from the same position. I had been with this gun only a short time, but I thought I had a very fine crew.

It was tiresome to wear a gas mask at all times so we arranged for one man to watch for gas shells and to blow a whistle when he saw one. Our masks did not let enough air through the filter to allow for quick or prolonged labor.

I soon found out that we were too heavy for side roads and that limited our movement quite a bit. The highways always were under fire, and every morning going out or coming back at night, we had to run the gauntlet. It was no use staying after dark and we were most anxious to return to our comfortable quarters where warm food was waiting. We would stop and listen, trying to find out the enemy's firing pattern for that day before we would attempt getting over the one-mile run of open road to the other side in one piece. There always came a time when the enemy gunners had to relax, and that was the time to have a heavy foot on the gas pedal. Twenty-five miles per hour was our top speed. But often there seemed to be no pattern to their firing and we just could not wait long enough to discover one. We had to go through, hoping for the best.

Once I was sitting in the front seat next to the chauffeur whose name was Rupp. He was a racing driver by profession and a very cool customer. We were sitting almost on top of the engine and the roar made it impossible to hear an explosion, even if it occurred 50 yards away. Not hearing gave us a feeling of security. A false one, I knew, but it helped. Our ears were stuffed with cotton. Without it our eardrums would have been damaged in no time.

I remember our first casualty on one of these runs. I had noticed nothing unusual when the man sitting behind me tapped me on the shoulder, pointing to one of the men whose jaw seemed to be shot away completely. I did not know what hit him, but we had to turn around and try to save his life by getting him to a dressing station quickly. That experience took the fun out of this proposition and from then on we became more apprehensive. To get the man to safety forced us to run the gauntlet four times that day. I began to admire the driver. To go at full speed over the open road offered the best security, but avoiding the shell craters required top skill. He would either straddle or let one wheel drop into the crater and when that was impossible, he would go on at full speed while the rest of us held on for dear life. At times it felt as if the whole truck and gun were jumping up, down and sideways. Why we never turned over on these wild rides was hard to figure out.

It was never long before somebody from the infantry appeared, asking us to shoot at ruins visible on the other side of No Man's Land. They said they had received mortar fire, there was a machine-gun nest, or they wanted something shot up for some other reason. I never could see anything and was not in favor of extracurricular shooting. We might have provoked heavy retaliation and that sort of useless banging away served no purpose. After a few days I claimed a shortage of ammunition when we received these requests. Besides, I was anxious to have enough ammo for a real emergency. On this front both sides often launched surprise attacks without artillery preparation. All hell could break loose at any time and a local fight could mean the beginning of large scale operations. Surprise was considered imperative for success, and nobody could feel at ease. So far our most active day was February 5. We saw plenty of targets and fired 248 rounds.

The newspapers reported that some sort of peace had been arranged with Russia, permitting transfer of about 80 combat divisions to the Western Front. For the first time I felt optimistic. Perhaps we could win and end this war soon. The fact that we would attack soon, pressing for a final decision, was common knowledge. No more leaves were granted. An army order stated everbody had to fight. Regimental and other offices doing paperwork would be closed. There would be no more soft jobs for anybody.

Our enemies, no doubt, knew what was coming, but I was astonished at how quiet the front was. All units were conserving their strength and ammunition except in the air, where wild melees high up could be seen every day.

The regular army captain commanding our group liked me for some reason. He said we probably would be in the first or second attacking division and if I wanted to see my family or wife, he could arrange a three-day leave for me. That was not time enough to go to Bremen so Dorothy and I met in Cologne. I did not tell her of coming events.

On my return I was ordered to man an observation post for a few days with a communication officer from one of the many fighter squadrons operating in the sector. This man, a First Lieutenant von Zastrow, belonged to the Richthofen outfit and I found him to be a very nice fellow. * From the first moment we met in the little hut with a corrugated tin roof, he was flabbergasted by the "shocking" lack of everything we was used to in the villa where the fighter pilots lived.

"Nagel, for heaven's sake, where do we eat, and wash and who makes our beds? Where are the beds? My God, this is terrible....." It was very amusing to me and we laughed a good deal. But this fellow soon had established connection with von Richthofen's headquarters by telephone, giving it a long list of things he urgently needed for survival. He had been a pilot and now had this communication job. His father was the commanding general of Berlin's garrison troops.

Nearby fighter squadrons wanted to know immediately whenever enemy planes crossed our lines in force. It was this man's job to figure out how this could be done. What I had to do with it I never knew. Per-

---

* Through correspondence, Nagel further identified this officer as **Oberleutnant** Hellmuth von Zastrow. Von Zastrow had entered the German Air Service at war's outbreak and flew on the Eastern Front with **Flieger-Bataillon Nr. 1** in late 1914 and early 1915. Commissioned a **Leutnant** in February 1915, he was transferred in May to the Champagne in France where he served as a pilot in **Fliegerabteilung 60**. During the battles about Verdun in 1916, von Zastrow flew a Fokker Eindecker as a scout and escort pilot. On August 26, 1916, he was transferred to **Jagdstaffel 2** as Oswald Boelcke's adjutant, a position held while Boelcke revamped German fighter aviation in the summer and fall of 1916, until the latter was killed accidentally on October 28, 1916. Von Zastrow was promoted to **Oberleutnant** in early 1917. From that time until the end of the war he served with the Office of the Inspector General for Air in Berlin. When Nagel met him, he presumably was providing communication service for von Richthofen's **Jagdgeschwader 1**, under the aegis of the Inspector General's office. Von Zastrow survived the war, but died a short time afterward of depression and illness. — R.A.B.

haps the group commander did not know what to do with me for a few days. While my new friend did his job, he kept up a steady barrage of complaints with very good results. Within hours a truck arrived with camp beds, blankets, food, wine and all kinds of other nice things, including playing cards. We were not in a very safe place — the tin roof offered no protection — and whenever we heard an explosion, he was anxious to know what probably would happen next. I do not believe he was afraid, but he never had been in the front lines before and did not hide his feelings by saying he thought this sort of life was quite awful. After a few days we were ordered back to our outfits.

On March 6 a nearby ammunition dump was hit and exploded, showering outfits in the surrounding area with debris. On March 10 very heavy shells suddenly hit a battery which we first had noticed in our sector a few days before. Within minutes it had 10 dead and 42 wounded. It seemed the situation was getting more tense every day. I had orders not to fire more than 50 rounds a day, except in grave emergencies, and that meant I only could shoot at planes coming over close by. Coming back at night to our quarters I could see the landscape crawling with newly-arrived soldiers. Every house and every bivouac area was filled up. That many soldiers just could not be hidden. The enemy knew what to expect, except the exact place of attack. The captain told me that in our sector three divisions would attack after an all-night artillery bombardment. I was to remain in my quarters as a reserve until further notice. A newly-arrived lieutenant would command K Flak 82 during the first assault, advancing as our infantry advanced and protecting them from enemy planes as best it could.

Breakthrough

I spent the night before the attack in a very agreeable and comfortable fashion. The various officers of our group were quartered in a large house where we found a good piano. We all had our orders. Some had to leave that same night to join their outfits; others, like me, were kept in reserve. The piano was a great and unexpected attraction for the music lovers among us. One of the lieutenants had a fine baritone voice. His deputy was the director of the Kiel Philharmonic Orchestra and as we soon found out, a very fine musician. To top it all, this man, half an hour before, had met a former violinist of his orchestra outside our quarters. He was a noncombatant and worked in a field hospital nearby. Everyone was delighted to hear good music again. They had no notes, but until after midnight, the baritone sang beautiful German Lieders and excerpts from Wagner's operas, accompanied perfectly on the piano by the orchestra leader who seemed able to play anything in all keys. The violinist performed a beautiful rendition of Bach's Chaconne, a violin piece to be played as a solo. Once that evening I tried to play a little on his violin, but it sounded embarrassingly amateurish and I soon gave it up.

During the pauses while all this lovely music was being played, we were quite aware that the enormous preparations for the next morning's attack were in full swing. We could hear the clatter of marching troops on the street outside and the constant RRHUM, RRHUM of the heavy artillery. Our windows never stopped rattling.

We did not know it then, but this orchestra leader evidently was an important person in musical circles. He was most delightful, friendly and humorous, willing to play anything to entertain us. A few days later he was mortally wounded. Telegrams from well known musical leaders poured in, among them one from Prince Heinrich, the brother of the Kaiser. He wanted him transported to Kiel, the main port of the German navy, where Prince Heinrich was an admiral. But this very nice fellow died. I can remember what he looked like, but I cannot remember his name.

That night I went to bed very comfortably, although it was late, around 2 a.m., and I wondered whether the constant and very heavy rattling of the windows would finally break them.

I hardly had gone to sleep when I had to get up because orders reached me to proceed to the observation post near Aubencheul and wait there for further orders. Nearby Malincourt was under heavy fire, but things were peaceful where I was.

The attack had started in the morning and soon news began to filter through. We already had advanced six kilometers and were now attacking the last British trenches before reaching open ground. Things looked good to me. Late in the morning the group commander sent his personal car with a chauffeur to bring me to K Flak 82. The lieutenant who had temporarily replaced me had been severely wounded (he lost his leg but lived), and the next in rank, a sergeant, also was badly hurt. An officer was needed in a hurry. The driver showed me on a map where we could expect to find the gun on the road to Albert just a few miles in front of us. As long as we stayed on the main road we could not miss it. It was a comfortable ride physically but otherwise quite horrible. We could move forward only at a snail's pace, stopping every few minutes. The road in front of us was stopped up — by what we did not know. What almost made me sick was the traffic to the left of us coming back from the battle zone. It moved very slowly and I barely could stand the sight. Many of the vehicles were horsedrawn forage wagons and I believe they were put into service at the last moment when casualties began to exceed expectations. All of them were filled with severly wounded men lying motionless, pale and bloody looking. I had seen many wounded before, but not in such an awful parade, one vehicle after another without end. The sight shook me up and I became frightened. After a while I forced myself to look away. The driver, meanwhile, seemed relaxed and smoked a cigar. I wondered whether he could take that sort of thing better than I. A thought struck me. The majority of these victims of high international politics came from the lower strata of our society: laborers, craftsmen, storekeepers, students and those too young to be classified yet. Win or lose, would their lives really change? Would their struggle for a meager living be easier or worse? In my opinion, if they survived they would come back to the same hard life they lived before. Not many Germans would gain anything from a victory as far as their personal lives and happiness were concerned. Neither could I feel that a defeat would cause misery all around. People still would go on living and working.

The roar of the battle in front of us became more distinct. Finally we came to a crossroads and I was astonished to see a colonel of the general staff, recognizable by the broad red stripes on his pants, coolly trying to regulate the traffic jam. Only combat troops and material badly needed could proceed. Everything else had to wait on the side roads. Engineers stood by to help pull stalled wagons into an open field. There was no time for hesitation. A few miles further on the battle had reached a critical stage and this colonel had to decide quickly what was to go through.

Looking around I saw dead horses still in harness and was told the situation in the early morning hours had been very desperate, hence the presence of this officer who belonged to the brain elite of the army. When the attack started, British heavy artillery kept this main road under fire, causing severe casualties among the troops moving forward. At times it was impossible for them to reach their forward positions at the right time. When our car arrived on the scene, enemy artillery fire on the road had slackened considerably. The enemy was retreating slowly and during a backward movement it was virtually impossible for their artillery to maintain the same volume of fire as when standing still. Most of the British artillery was horsedrawn and it took time for them to find a suitable new position, get the range and open up again, this quite apart from the fact that our artillery managed to keep up an enormous bombardment. The screeching of heavy shells over our heads never stopped.

The weather remained good and early that afternoon I finally found K Flak 82 on the main highway near Bony-St. Emiel. The loss of the lieutenant and sergeant in the morning had shaken up the crew and they were a quiet bunch of soldiers when I joined them. Earlier, while moving forward with the attacking infantry, shells exploded all around them, splinters first hitting the lieutenant and a little later, the sergeant. But now, they explained, the situation was easier.

Looking to the right and left I could see thousands of our infantry moving forward over the fields, walking at a steady pace. The rumbling of our motor, plus the cotton in my ears, transformed the noise of battle into one confused roar. I could not tell where the noise was coming from, but I clearly could see what was going on. Puffs of exploding shrapnel and geysers of earth from exploding shells of all calibers amidst our advancing lines seemed to be everywhere. Men were going down, whether to take cover or because they were hit I could not tell. We were fighting over a pretty landscape of slightly rolling hills dotted with houses and clumps of trees. Just how heavy the enemy infantry fire was I could not determine either, but I was convinced our infantry was having a hell of a time.

We rolled along but did not contribute much to the battle. Royal Flying Corps planes seemed to be everywhere and tried to stop the advance. Most of the time they were too low for us, zooming down with machine-guns going full blast, and never high enough to become safe targets. We could not fire on a plane operating over the heads of our own men. The chances of hitting such fast-moving targets were practically nil, while the danger of hitting our soldiers and showering them with splinters was great. Ordinarily, good anti-aircraft fire forced the enemy to fly high, but this was a life or death struggle and these RFC fliers continued to dive in regardless of the risk. Only a direct hit could stop them. We advanced slowly until sundown, when we found a cluster of trees where we could spend the night.

All of us were very tired and I thought the safest place to sleep would be under the vehicle. The truckbed and wheels would protect us fairly well from stray shots. Nearby I saw some 10 or 15 dead English soldiers. German soldiers had ransacked their pockets. Letters and playing cards were strewn all over the place. I read many of these letters, all written by seemingly simple British people, complaining of wartime restrictions and ordinary family affairs, but all asking when they could expect the soldier home. I took some of these letters with me. Perhaps I could write the families when all this was over, but none had a return address.

For the next two days it was more of the same. We were near Peronne on the Somme River and I felt enemy resistance was becoming heavier, especially their artillery fire. Shells exploded too close for comfort and we had to duck or jump in the ditch quite often, though we managed to get through safely.

On March 24 we got into another incredible traffic jam. I had no idea what had caused it, but our K Flak was jammed in tight between horse-drawn field artillery. This time British planes came roaring in, four or five at a time, strafing without mercy. None of our fighters were in sight. We had to open up and fire as best we could right over the heads of men and horses only a few feet away. Nearby infantry let go with machine-guns. With few interruptions these fights and attacks continued all day long.

To the left of us was the usual procession of the Red Cross vehicles. While we worried about the danger of these constant attacks from the air, I wondered how a wounded man must have felt, completely helpless in those wagons while machine-gun bullets spattered all around.

During a halt in the afternoon, we located what looked like a fine

British truck about 20 yards away on a sideroad. It was covered and looked like something we would love to have. Curiously enough, the motor was still running. There was a little blood on the seat, but our chauffeur pronounced it a wonderful find. Inside were cans of gas, a small field bed, some tea, bread and biscuits. It looked too good to be true and we were determined to annex it. At night we could sleep in it, out of the weather. We had to act fast. The chauffeur would drive the truck and squeeze it into the traffic behind our gun, which I would drive. But I was a very poor driver by standards of today, and when the traffic moved again I felt uneasy. I was not sure what the dials on the instrument panel meant and I did not know if I could stop properly and quickly. Shifting the heavy gears was no easy matter for a beginner in a constant traffic jam. For a while things went well — until I found myself driving just behind a horsedrawn infantry kitchen. It consisted of an iron kettle with a fire grate underneath, surrounded by a narrow platform on which the cook stood. I knew I was too close but I could not help it. When the next stop came I could not find the brakes fast enough. The cook jumped off his platform and I ran smack into the steaming kettle, hard enough to make a disagreeable grinding noise and smash the wooden platform, bending the kettle slightly. A company commander soon appeared and shouted for quite a while. I could understand none of it while the motor was roaring. I made signs of apology and only then did he notice I was an officer of the same rank. Perhaps he remembered it was not customary for one lieutenant to ball out another one. At any rate, there was no time for long arguments and this crisis also passed by.

Moving along slowly on the main highway a little later, there appeared to the right of us a huge complex of large, circus-like tents. I felt certain it was some sort of British supply depot, possibly supplying the whole British 5th Army. I motioned to the chauffeur driving the truck behind us, pointing to the tents. He understood immediately. I told one of the crew to jump on the truck and help load anything we could use or eat. The column moved forward very slowly, but after some 30 minutes, we had passed the depot and I worried how the truck could ever catch up with us. About an hour later we came to a country crossroad and to my surprise, there was the truck waiting for us, the chauffeur grinning all over his face. The soldier jumped back on the gun and told us they had loaded many cases of the most wonderful things to eat: condensed milk, tea, cocoa, corned beef, sugar, bacon, tinned butter, cookies, biscuits and countless cartons of English Woodbine cigarettes. To convince us of his tale he had stuffed his pockets with cigarettes and cookies. They also brought an armful of raincoats made out of real rubber — something very scarce in Germany. Our mouths watered and we were most anxious for night to fall so we could stuff ourselves with these incredible goodies. It was a treasure beyond price. We were always hungry and completely sick of army slop. That evening some of the soldiers drank the first cup of real cocoa they had tasted in years. I loaded up on biscuits and jam, plus tea and milk, and then stretched out on the English field bed.

We hardly had made a dent in our supplies when we began to worry that some staff officer might order the truck off the road as unnecessary baggage. But, all in all, it had been a good day and we were looking forward to an elegant breakfast with coffee and bacon. My men began stirring when it was still pitch dark. They were hungry and could not wait. Before we moved on we tried to hide the food under the gasoline cans. Somebody might look in and confiscate our treasures.

The forward drive continued, though very slowly. We were still on the main highway, but soon I felt that we had to get off this road or be blown to bits. I knew our captain well enough to know his orders to proceed on the main road need not be followed if circumstances made it impossible. Much later on I read that on the fifth day of this battle, the British 5th Army had received heavy artillery reinforcements from the French. Judging from the blasts now hitting us I thought their artillery must be massed wheel to wheel. And the types of shells coming over had changed, too. It was possible to hear a 75 mm. or a 10 cm. shell coming, but the heavy caliber shells came over with enormous speed, without warning, and exploded with a shattering noise in a blinding blaze of light. We could not move forward while tons of steel splinters were zooming all around us. We stopped and jumped in a narrow ditch, which felt like a haven of safety. There was no escape from such a barrage. We could survive only if we managed to drive quickly somewhere else presently not under fire.

As I looked out of the ditch, I saw that the artillery and infantry had left the highway and were scattered over the neighboring fields to escape the shelling. The highway now seemed more or less free. We jumped on the gun and dashed off with our precious truck behind us. I never had driven the gun at top speed, but all I could do was put my foot down and let her go. Nobody was hit and that astonished me, but I could not find a sideroad. After driving forward for a few minutes we caught up with a regiment of infantry marching along without being molested by artillery. Looking behind we still could see geysers of dirt shooting up as high as trees.

So far we had advanced about 10 miles and the town of Albert was in front of us, some five miles away. Our territorial gains already exceeded those made by the massive French and British attacks mounted during the previous two years. But, to me, our slow and very bloody progress did not look like a breakthrough, nor could I detect the slightest sign of a British collapse. Judging from the many dead and the never-ending stream of wounded coming back, it was evident the enemy had no idea of quitting. The British and French were throwing in all their reserves regardless of losses, knowing that fresh American divisions were now ready to relieve the French near Metz so French troops could be moved north to stop our drive. That the enemy became stronger every day could be felt clearly.

On March 26 a heavy battery near us began bombarding Albert from 12 kilometers away. The latest army paper reported that a newly constructed heavy gun, the "Big Bertha," was shelling Paris from a distance of 75 miles. Although nobody got hurt on the 26th — and that was a miracle — it was a trying day.

Early in the morning a motorcycle rider brought an order to abandon the truck. It was needed for more important duties. I knew we could not keep it long so it was important to load all of our treasures onto the gun truck, and that was not easy. Our pockets were stuffed and the rest of the biscuits and tin cans rolled around on the floor.

It now seemed our forward drive had stopped completely. All we could do was to move sideways within our sector. The battle had become a slugging match. Shells of all calibers slammed into the landscape without letup. Every half hour or so we darted off to take a new position somewhere near, always hoping it might be better there.

Air targets were plentiful and we fired whenever we could, though it did not seem to make much difference. Enemy planes were surrounded quickly by hundreds of black explosion puffs coming from all directions. According to rumors, we had massed 1,000 anti-aircraft guns for this drive. We saw a few planes shot down, but not many. Victims of air fights were much more numerous.

Both sides had observation balloons up in full force. The whole front was lined with them. On our side each balloon was protected by several small-bore cannon, able to throw up a stream of oversized machine-gun bullets. Inspite of this protection, burning balloons were a common sight. Looking up, one would not have to wait long to see a German or British balloon come down. It only took one hit of a tracer bullet to cause an explosion.

In this battle we labored under considerable stress and strain, but my relations with the crew remained excellent. It may have taken longer to become an officer in the German army, but once the rank had been obtained, there was no need to assert authority because it never was challenged. The soldiers felt their officers must know more than they or they would not be officers. Of course, there were exceptions among officers of the reserve in the rear echelons. Many had been made officers 25 years before the war. The small, so-called military courtesies always were observed under all conditions. Nobody would address me except in the third person. Personally, I would not have cared how they addressed me, but any deviation from accepted form and discipline would have shocked me, signifying a very serious breakdown.

Late the afternoon of the 26th, another motorcycle messenger brought orders for me to appear at K Flak headquarters, together with officers from batteries belonging to the same group. After sundown a small car picked me up. The purpose of the meeting was to allocate territories for the K Flak to operate in. I received orders to remain in my sector and then to proceed to Albert by sunrise to protect our lines against interference from the air. Albert had been taken, it was said, late on the 26th. I probably would find our lines several kilometers outside of town.

The same car took me back and before I went to sleep next to the driver, I remembered our cozy English truck was no more and I would have to sleep in the open again. When I woke up our car had stopped on a dark road with the lights out. The driver was lost and I had no idea where we were. Flares and gunfire were all around us and we could not tell where our lines should be. What astonished us was the absence of soldiers. Nobody could be seen and that was not normal at all. We had to be in No Man's Land. It was dark but we could see the trees and some distance down the road. After anxious waiting we heard voices mixed with a few loud commands coming from a road nearby. We could not tell whether they spoke German or English, so we stood still, hoping something would happen to help us. Fortunately, neither side wished to waste ammunition on this No Man's Land road. However, it was certain we had to get away before sunrise. Finally we made up our minds and decided to turn to the left, going very slowly with lights out. After crawling along for some 15 minutes, the driver suddenly recognized a landmark. From then on things went smoothly and when I stretched out under the gun truck about midnight, I was too tired to worry about anything.

Streetfighting in Albert

March 27 was a typical March day — cold and foggy. We broke camp before sunup and arrived in front of Albert about 6 a.m. According to my dictionary, the town of Albert had some 7,500 inhabitants and looked similar to other French country towns.

My orders here were to concentrate on low-flying British battle fliers who already had inflicted serious losses on our advancing troops. The Richthofen fighter group was operating over Albert and we could see his men doing their best all day, but it looked as if nobody had the upperhand. Air fights never ceased. The sky over Albert was the stage for the most determined air battles I ever saw. Nobody gave an inch. Only lack of sufficient machine-gun bullets could induce a fighter to break away. Both sides were willing to fight it out right then and there, win or lose. I could not tell how many planes were lost on both sides. It did not make much difference anyway as fresh fighter planes would take the places of ones lost. This battle came to an end only because the sun went down for the day.

While these fights went on at high altitudes, low-flying planes on each side worked on the opposing infantry and artillery without being disturbed from above. These battle planes flew so low I often thought they would crash, when suddenly they reappeared skimming the treetops. I knew they were lightly armored underneath, but I still could not understand how so many managed to survive. Those fights were really wild.

Shortly after entering Albert, we sensed that something was wrong and we became apprehensive. If the town already had been taken, where were the soldiers? The streets were empty and houses were closed. They showed very little damage. It looked as if we were the only ones in town. I expected to find the streets filled with marching troops and vehicles of all descriptions. Perhaps we were in No Man's Land. Or, perhaps the British had withdrawn without fighting, laying a huge trap for our troops to come in, only to be encircled for the final kill. What handicapped me was the fact my hearing seemed impaired. Except for very loud bangs close to me I did not hear well enough to draw conclusions. Was the battle noise near us? I could not understand the situation, but decided to go on slowly.

Turning a corner we saw soldiers in position lying on the pavement across the street some 50 yards or so in front of us. We stopped and I went toward them to gather information, but as I approached, I saw they were dead. We had to move them to a sidewalk before we could proceed. Now I was sure we had not yet reached our line. A little further down the street we encountered a wounded German Marine propped against a house. He was shot through the foot and told us the British were "just around that corner." When I looked I could not see the enemy and decided to go on. The noise of our motor was most annoying and I wished I could hear something. A few minutes later, a German soldier came out of one of the houses lining the street and frantically waved us back. He seemed most anxious for us to understand that we were in grave danger unless we moved back immediately. It all seemed very queer so, leaving our gun behind, I walked toward him. He motioned to walk close to the houses and not in the middle of the sidewalk. He also shouted, explaining that British soldiers still were holding houses at the end of the street. I thought this situation was very dangerous, but I could not understand why nobody was fighting.

Across this narrow street seemed to be a headquarters. An officer appeared waving for me to come over, which I did, running fast and keeping my head low. I still did not quite understand the overall situation and was glad to meet somebody who could explain it.

The captain introduced himself as the commander of the 3rd Battalion of the 1st Marine Infantry Regiment. Its men were known in the army as top-notch soldiers. What astonished me so was the enthusiasm with which this captain received me. He pumped my hand and thanked me profusely for coming to his aid. This introduction took place while both of us were crouching on the floor of the little house. The windows were broken and he urged me not to stick my head above the window sills because the British were still in the garden. This man was a professional, very polite and soft-spoken, and I knew he would not exaggerate. He offered me some wine and then began explaining.

They had been in this battle since the 21st and hoped to be relieved soon because they had reached the end of their strength. Albert had been taken the day before without too much trouble, but now, at this edge of town, they had encountered fierce resistance which had to be overcome before the battalion could break out into the open fields as ordered. The 3rd Battalion had attacked the day before, March 26, without success and suffered terrible losses. Many of the companies now were commanded by non-coms. Most of its casualties were caused by a machine-gun nest installed in a factory building about 400 yards in front of our line.

That this captain and the men milling around in his headquarters were utterly exhausted could be seen easily. But they had orders to attack again at 8 a.m. The captain could see only complete failure and very bloody losses ahead of him as long as that machine-gun nest dominated the sector. The windows of the nest were well protected by sandbags and machine-guns had been placed in all six windows, easily visible through binoculars. Artillery was needed to knock them out, but supporting artillery was nowhere in sight. Now, quite unexpectedly, we had arrived on the scene with a field artillery gun. When I asked the captain why enemy artillery was not in action, he explained they did not dare shoot as long as the lines were so close together.

The captain asked one of his aides to take me to the roof of the house so I could see the layout clearly. While going up I wanted to say something, but my guide put his finger to his lips, asking me to be very quiet. The steep roof had a small window flush with it, which had to be raised by pushing it up. This we did slowly, trying to make no noise. When I looked out I was flabbergasted to see the flat tin hats of British infantry below us in the garden only 50 yards away. The enemy seemed to be everywhere — some in foxholes, some in short trenches, some hidden behind trees, hedges and so on. What I saw was not a fixed line. We could not tell exactly where their line began or where it stopped, but we were certain an attack would be a desperate undertaking.

Coming down from the roof I tried to explain our limitations. We were an anti-aircraft gun operating under orders of the Air Service, I told the captain, and ill-equipped for ground fighting. We did not have a protective shield like the field artillery. I realized I could not ignore the wishes of this battalion, quite apart from the fact the captain could order me to do anything he wanted. This was a desperate combat situation and I would have to obey. Something had to be done before 8 a.m. when the new attack would have to start.

Before going on with my story I want to describe the general atmosphere prevailing on the 27th.

We had learned that morning that the British soldiers opposing us in Albert had been replaced overnight by a fresh Australian division, while replacements for our side did not show up. Our supporting artillery could not get through the traffic jam. Our right flank touched the left flank of the 248th Infantry Regiment. The infantry was dead tired. We felt somewhat better because every night so far we had managed to get some sleep, although the nights were now cold. But the fighting became more ferocious by the hour, as shown by these excerpts from diaries of officers and men who survived this battle, published in book form after the war. The following happened to a battalion of the 248th Regiment, which was to the right of us and well supported by field artillery:

> At about 5:30 p.m., a plane drops a message saying that tanks are coming over the hill to our left. The field artillery resting 500 yards behind us is now coming forward, taking firing positions for our protection. It is their plan to let the tanks advance as near as possible. The battery opens fire on the first tank crawling over the hill, which keeps coming, firing with its cannon and machine-gun. At 750 yards it gets hit and seems to explode. The crew jumps out, runs a few yards, then collapses. The other tanks move on until hit. But three tanks remain untouched and now are trying to encircle the remaining two guns. The crews of the other two guns have been killed or wounded during the last 10 minutes. At this moment the lieutenant commanding is hit and goes down. Of the three tanks two more are hit but are able to leave the field under their own power. Now only one tank is boring in and only one gun is left to oppose it. On this gun all are dead or wounded, except two gunners. They pretend to be dead. The tank moves on to crush the gun, but when within 30 yards these two men jump up, hitting the tank with the last shell they had left.

On the same afternoon, a member of the 248th Regiment's 2nd Battalion reported in his diary about the death of an artillery officer. His battery still was stalled somewhere in the rear, but he had gone forward to look over the situation.

> The attack of our battalion surprised the enemy and we were able to take five officers and 129 men as prisoners. They surrendered their weapons, but a moment after throwing down their guns, they grabbed them again and a murderous man-to-man fight started. After we had killed their commanding officer they gave up, but during the melee the artillery officer fell mortally wounded.

The above events were typical of the battle in and around Albert. Both sides were desperate for victory. Human lives were cheap; nobody gave it a thought.

While talking to the Marine captain about the plans to eliminate the enemy machine-gun nest, a soldier brought a message stating that a Canadian officer had been taken prisoner by the neighboring battalion. During his interrogation he had expressed with complete confidence his conviction that our next attack would fail. He had talked of "hundreds of machine-gun nests which had been constructed last night....." The captain believed him, but thought these fortifications probably were a little further back where the terrain was more favorable for defense.

During the last hour before the ordered attack, I was anxious to get all the information I could, and at the same time, explain the maximum help we could render.

According to the book, the best way to knock out the nest was by indirect fire, shooting from some place not visible to the enemy. That was impossible. To do so, the gun would have to be pulled back, perhaps to the marketplace in the middle of the town, hidden under some trees if possible. Then I would have had to go forward to where I could see the target and direct the firing by telephone. But we had no telephone or telephone wire with us. The skies were full of enemy fliers and this was not the time for a leisurely turkey shoot. After the first few shots we would get plenty of bombs from above and the final result would have been much in doubt. This approach also would take too long, even if we could find a field telephone somewhere. That house could be eliminated only by direct fire and when I explained this to the captain, he wanted me to do it right away. The sooner those machine-guns were out of the way, the better, he said. I became embarrassed because I had to explain again that we could not possibly succeed that way. Our Nr. 1 gunner had to see the target clearly and he could see it only if we left the protection of the house we were hiding behind. The minute our gun barrel was visible to the Australian riflemen — some only 50 yards away — they would fill us full of lead before we could fire our first shot. I was greatly relieved when he agreed with me. I told him the best way to help would be for us to roll forward with his attack, shooting as we went, hoping to hit the nest before it could do too much damage. The captain did not like this plan very much, fearing we would be too big and slow a target. In his opinion, we would be exposed to very heavy rifle fire, especially if we failed to knock down the house with the machine-guns quickly. I knew very little about this sort of fighting and I was anxious to benefit from this man's experience.

It seemed that losses always became intolerable as soon as an attack stopped. Rifle fire, mortars and field artillery then would zero in and once they had the range, men would go down in droves. According to the captain, the only thing to do was to get up and advance. The enemy would shoot well and calmly from a comfortable distance, he said, but losses would diminish the faster we attacked. During the last 100 yards the enemy would fire too high. He had no time to adjust his sights. That sounded plausible and finally we agreed on a hit-and-run attack. All this talk was nice enough, but the whole thing was rather terrifying. I did not want to speculate on our chances for survival. I was apprehensive and my pulse probably was not normal, though I felt I could manage all right. I wished to be somewhere else, but I discarded those thoughts as completely useless.

If speed was a life-saving factor, then we would manage well because speed was our forte. I thought it best not to explain the plan in detail to the whole crew. The driver, however, had to play a major role. From the roof I let him see the road we had to travel. The house we wanted to demolish could be seen clearly, some 400 yards away and about 20 yards to the left of the road. Half way was a country crossroad. We had to advance to there, but not farther, because we needed the crossroad to turn around. Arriving at the crossroad, we would have to fire point blank and hit the house quickly. We could not survive a drawn-out fight with several machine-guns and all those Australian riflemen. We had to operate fast, I emphasized. The driver understood perfectly and assured me he would get us in and out without fail. Of course, we both understood that we would advance at full speed as soon as the Marines started their attack, and at the rate of 25 miles per hour, we would be way in the rear of the Australians within minutes. According to the captain, the enemy would be too rattled to turn around and attack us. His men would take care of that, he assured me.

It was now about half an hour before zero hour. The crew knew we would join in the coming attack and would try to knock out machine-guns. They were ordered to set 12 shells at point-blank range. Each man of the loading crew was to have one shell under his arm ready to load with the utmost speed. The Nr. 1 gunner was the one operating the sights. Our Nr. 1 was a quiet, dependable boy who never talked much. He did his duty like an expert. I often thought that his speed in getting a target into the sights was astonishing. It was his duty to get the house squarely into his sights before he shouted "Ready," and he understood the importance of it. He knew we could not afford to miss at a range of 200 yards. I now believed our surprise attack would succeed, but I could not figure out how we would manage to get back. After raising hell on that battlefield with the only gun on our side, we would be a target as big as a barn door.

About 15 minutes before zero hour our heavy artillery started a bombardment. It seemed to fall all along the line. Perhaps the whole Second Army would attack now. The big shells coming from somewhere behind us made a constant humming noise. Some seemed to shriek as if they were tumbling over in the air. Salvo after salvo exploded on the other side. The geysers of mud and debris could be seen easily, but we were disappointed because none of the shells landed among the enemy directly in front of us. Our artillery tried to seal off the battlefield so reinforcements could not come through.

On the hour, the Marines started the attack and that was our cue. I had forgotten to ask the captain about enemy mines and that bothered me. But off we went. Out of the corner of my eye I could see Marines coming out of houses, foxholes and trenches in great numbers. I vaguely wondered where they all came from.

The crossroad was reached very quickly and the gun was loaded. Shortly before the takeoff I had told the Nr. 2 gunner, who pulled the trigger, to be careful and not shoot before the chauffeur and I had jumped off the front seats. I had tried to make a little joke about what would happen if he shot our heads off, but I guess I was not funny. Nobody felt like laughing.

My feet barely had touched the ground when our first shell came screaming out of the barrel. The flash and crack almost flattened me. The crew reloaded, fired, reloaded, fired, reloaded and fired again with amazing speed. Nobody had time to watch the target except me. Glancing back, I saw the Nr. 1 gunner had been hit and fall from his seat, bleeding. But the gun sights were set and new shells were jammed into the barrel before the recoils ended. By this time I already had seen that the very first shell had slammed right into the nest, as did every one of the following shots. Men could be seen jumping out of the windows. The house seemed to explode and started to burn. The target existed no more. It had been quite easy.

The loss of these machine-guns must have been a blow to the Australians. Perhaps they did not know what to make of us, or they did not realize we had a field gun aboard, but they knew now. The first shot of ours had made me almost deaf. As the small arms fire reached a crescendo, I could not make out whether they were shooting at us, except that a rifle bullet had knocked off one of our gunners. Waving my arm to follow me, the crew jumped into a ditch, half carrying the wounded man with them. He still could move a little under his own power.

My only thought was to get out of there. To do it quickly was imperative. I could not see how the fight was going. Did our men catch up with us or were we still behind the Australian front lines? If so, one hand grenade would have finished us off. One man had dressed the gunner's wound and it did not appear that he was badly hurt, although I could not be sure. I was anxious to get him to a dressing station.

What bothered us the most now was the fact the gun was pointed in the wrong direction. It had to be turned around. To go back and reach the safety of the first house 200 yards away in reverse gear would not be possible because the truck was too slow. We would never make it and stay alive. I was convinced our luck could not last much longer. We were in a tight spot. Tiny bits of flying earth and rock told us the rifle fire still was heavy, making it risky to try returning on foot. I had no clear idea where the enemy was and I did not know what to do next.

At that instant, Rupp the chauffeur shouted something into my ear which I could not understand. The next moment he cranked up the motor, jumped on and turned the truck around while the rest of us held our breath. As he came alongside our ditch, we jumped on, too. I never have understood why nobody got hurt on that wild ride. One machine-gun burst could have killed the driver who had to sit upright on his seat. The roar of battle made it quite impossible for us to hear whether bullets were zooming around us or not.

When we reached the safety of the first house we stopped and tried to relax. Our gunner's wound did not seem too bad. It looked as if the bullet had gone through his upper leg. Everybody seemed to be in high humor to have escaped alive. I thanked the chauffeur for what I thought

was a magnificent performance. He received the Iron Cross First
Class, the highest decoration a soldier below the rank of lieutenant
could obtain. I never had met such a character. He was about 35 years
old, much older than the rest of the crew. Whenever quick and resolute
action was required he was there to do it, and his loud laugh could be
heard at all times. Besides being a former racing driver he was a top-
notch mechanic and did all the repair work on the gun and motor. His
conversation was exclusively about racing, motors, women and more
women. While regaling those 20-year-old boys with his wild tales, they
wondered if so much could be true. But they admired him all the same.
I was lucky to have had him on the crew. Of the many people I met during four years of war, he was one of the few I can remember well: tall,
very strong looking, his face broad and red all over. Not brown but red.
When I asked him what had made him jump on the truck under those
very dangerous circumstances — probably saving our lives — his answer was, "The motor is in fine shape and I am not letting those
S.O.B.s shoot it up....."

Bagging a Bristol

It was now about 9:30 a.m. Before resuming our routine duty of
shooting at low-flying planes we had a good meal of corned beef and all
the other delicacies still on hand from our raid on the British supply depot a few days before.

Albert still looked empty with the exception of dressing stations established in cellars. We soon found ourselves in the marketplace. I was
looking for some open space from where we could operate without being hemmed in by houses, but shells came over too often for comfort. A
British shell had hit the golden Madonna on Albert's medieval church.
When we saw it she was hanging head down from a wire, as if plunging
to her death. It became a famous picture, published in many newspapers.

Cruising around Albert I talked to a Marine officer who said the attack of his division had petered out. Some ground had been taken, but
unless heavy reinforcements arrived quickly, he feared the Marines
would be pounded to pieces. So, the Canadian officer predicting failure
had been right.

In one of the town's side streets we saw a small but elegant looking
shoe store. For several years Albert had been occupied by British
troops and the high boots I saw in that store window looked very good to
me. Our shoes were always in bad shape because it was so difficult to
obtain new ones. We barely had entered when the ceiling seemed to collapse. Plaster and dust fell on us and we decided a small bomb or a
shell had hit next door. I saw no point in staying there any longer. A few
men grabbed some shoes while I took a very elegant cane that was

leaning against a counter. For some time it was my prized possession, but I lost it.

I thought it best to leave town and find an open field. But before we could do that, British battle fliers jumped us at exactly 10:10 a.m., according to my official report.

First, I saw explosions in front of us while we drove along one of the side streets, and I wondered where they came from. I did not believe at all that they were aimed at us. Then the man behind me touched my shoulder, drawing my attention to an explosion behind us. The dust was still settling. Looking up, several Bristol doubledeckers carrying two men and two machine-guns could be seen milling around over our heads, looking enormously big as they flew no more than 100 feet above us. I still was not certain whether they were after us or some other target. We stopped and I ordered the crew to take cover beneath the gun. We survived the next explosion, but it was awfully close. Perhaps it would have been better to run when we first saw these planes, but now we were in a tight spot again. One bomb hit would cause our ammo to explode. Given enough time they would finish us off for sure. There were four planes or more. Their speed must have been about 100 miles per hour and that was much too fast for aimed fire at so low a target.

After blowing "Man the gun!" on my whistle, the crew jumped on the truck under orders to set shrapnel at point blank range, maximum elevation straight up, load and wait for my signal for rapid fire. I was glad to have such a fine crew. They understood perfectly. When I saw the wings of the Bristols coming over the rooftops to my left, we blasted away so fast I thought the whole gun might topple over. Within seconds I saw one plane hit, coming down squarely as if it would fall on top of us. This episode took less time than it takes to write about it.

We were sure they would come back. I had to give no orders. The crew had reloaded and waited for my signal. Again they came over the rooftops. Fortunately, at the very last split second, I recognized that these planes were tripledeckers belonging to the Richthofen squadron. I was thankful the crew was disciplined enough not to have started firing before I could give the signal. To shoot down Richthofen, the national hero, would have been awful. However, he was not personally among these fliers who saved us. Within minutes the sky was clear. We were safe, but although we had shot down a plane, there was no elation. *
We were getting mighty tired and wondered if this sort of thing would go on all day long. I was looking for a place where we could spend the rest of the day in a less hectic manner, without being accused of running away.

* The RFC suffered a fairly high number of casualties on March 27, 1918, creating difficulties in determining the identity of the Bristol and its crew brought down by **K Flak 82**. This plane probably was a Bristol F2b Fighter, although Nagel refers to it as a "Bristol doubledecker." On this date, 10 two-seaters were reported lost by the RFC, while the Germans claimed 17 British two-seaters as shot down or forced to land. Of these, German pilots claimed a total of seven Bristol Fighters, and Flak units three, including Na-

Our driver had the same idea. Repairs on the motor had to be made before we could go out again, he said. The desire was overwhelming to sleep in that comfortable bed back in our old quarters where we started six days before. Since this offensive began the enemy had been pushed back 12 to 15 miles in our sector and no shells could reach us. Everybody washed up and once more I felt like a human being. Before going to bed, I sent the following report to Captain Specht, the group commander of K Flak Nr. 2:

Action of March 27, 1918.

I took a firing position at the east exit of Albert. Because the infantry was fighting without artillery support, I thought it best to support them, although enemy fliers were very active. After consulting with the battalion commander of the 3rd Battalion, 1st Marine Infantry Regiment, I proceeded to the exit on the highway Albert-Millencourt where we attacked a machine-gun nest that was especially harmful to our infantry. The house went up in flames after the fourth shot (incendiary shrapnel). We fired on the fleeing crews. As agreed upon with the leader of the attacking battalion we advanced on a sideroad. We succeeded in routing the enemy.

At 10:10 we were suddenly attacked by infantry fliers. We shot one down with the eighth shot.

Losses: One man wounded.

K Flak 82
Nagel
Lieutenant

The next day, March 28, again was rainy and cold and we made the best out of this period of rest. We knew that all divisions fighting since March 21 had been replaced and withdrawn for rest, but nobody seemed to think about withdrawing us for a little while. Air battles increased in ferocity and all K Flaks were needed. Richthofen's red plane could be seen every day in our sector. My diary reminded me of a story making the rounds at that time.

Baron Albrecht von Richthofen, the flier's father, was a retired major and too old for service. Just about this time, when the big air fights

gel's. The RFC/RAF War Diary shows the loss of only two Bristol Fighters that day — one from 20 Squadron and another from 11 Squadron. It is known that Manfred von Richthofen shot down the Bristol from 20 Squadron, but he also received credit for another Bristol F2b Fighter on the same day. According to Royal Flying Corps Communique No. 133, considerable activity in the air occurred over Albert on March 27, and involved both low level bombing missions and offensive fighter patrols. Of the latter, several were flown by members of Bristol-equipped 22 Squadron RFC, although this unit did not record any losses that day. As to the bombing raids mentioned in the War Diary for March 27, only 18 Squadron, flying D.H. 4s, lost an aircraft in the Albert area.

were a daily occurrence, he decided to visit his son. Permission was
granted. When he arrived at the airstrip of his son's squadron, none of
the fliers whose names he knew greeted him. They were up in the air
fighting over their own airfield against a swarm of Royal Flying Corps
fighters. Before he could pick up his bag, two of our fighters came sailing down, crashing right in front of him. That was too much for the old
man. He wanted to be taken home right away. It was the last time he
saw his son Manfred, who was shot down and killed a short time later.
Curiously enough, I always thought I had witnessed his last battle, but
checking on the dates, this was not so. I was in school in Lille.

For the first time since March 20 I saw the group commander. He
was extremely friendly and praised us. All this I could not quite understand, until he read to me a report received through channels from the
1st Marine Infantry Regiment, dated Albert, March 27, 9 a.m.

> The Lt. Nagel of K Flak 82 today advanced with his Autoflak to
> within about 200 yards of the first enemy line without seeking shel-
> ter, supporting the heavy fighting infantry by firing directly at ene-
> my machine-gun nests. He fought most successfully against low
> flying enemy planes. The commander and crew of the flak are fully
> deserving to be decorated because their performance must be de-
> scribed as quite outstanding.

> Signed: Engholm, Captain
> Commander 3rd Bat.
> Marine Inf. Regiment Nr. 1

After the war I was anxious to know whether this nice Marine captain had survived. Going over a list of 2,145 names listed as killed in action with the 1st Marine Regiment, I was glad when I did not find his
name.

Of course, all this noise about us pleased me very much and I hoped
my decoration would come through.

The next few days were routine but hard on our nerves. Albert was
crumbling under heavy bombardment so we tried to find some reasonably safe position near the town in one of the fields. It was cold, rainy
and wet. A fine drizzle never stopped and the idea of remaining out
there all day made us shiver. Most of the time we spent in little slit
trenches hastily dug, but good enough for protection. None of the heavy
shells came too close. Knowing that my stay in this sector would be
over very soon, I had no wish whatever playing the hero.

My last day here got us into contact with a very furious major. It was
foggy and impossible to see more than 20 yards or so. At one time I had
no idea where we were. I especially was afraid of gas shells, which
were impossible to see or hear exploding in foggy weather. As we stood
there everything was peaceful. No artillery or small arms fire could be
heard anywhere. Then, out of the fog came a major, all wrapped up in a
shawl. He stalked toward us through the mud, swinging his walking

cane in the air as one would when approaching a trespasser. He began shouting, but we had too much cotton in our ears to understand him. He still was shouting when within a yard of me, telling me to go away and to do so quickly. What could we do with that silly little gun? he asked. His men had suffered enough, he said, and when the fog lifted the enemy would zero in on us, but would hit his men in that trench, etc., etc. He threatened that his men would take potshots at us if we did not disappear right away. They would be furious, he emphasized. I tried to reason with him a little because, in the fog, I did not know where to go. But that man was hysterical. We left.

We still were operating in territory very recently evacuated by the enemy. His dugouts, equipment and shot-up wagons could be seen everywhere. Discarded rubber raincoats were in profusion. Looking around with my binoculars I saw a tidy-looking dugout with the door open some 50 yards away from us. It would offer excellent, dry shelter, so I went over to take a look. I had entered many of these enemy dugouts and was always impressed by the fact they were so poorly constructed compared to ours. It was as if the builders did not care. But this one looked good. It had a very small window in the rear, although the light was so dim I hardly could see. I was shocked when I saw two English officers at a table, one sleeping with his head on his arm and the other sitting straight up. Both had their caps on. This sudden confrontation stupified me. I stood there wondering if they would say ''Hello,'' when I realized they were dead. To see these men in that dim light, motionless and so rigid, made my heart pound. I left quickly. Once outside, I began to understand that something was wrong. Our infantry had not entered to look for food or good English shoes because the bodies were boobytrapped. How could a dead man sit upright on a chair? I clearly remember the gruesome atmosphere of that episode. When I told my driver about it, he, of course, was eager to go in there and get their shoes. He knew all about boobytraps, he said. Nothing doing, I told him.

One other thing also became clear. Germany was slowly but surely being starved. There was not enough substantial food to be had. The very small amounts of meat available for soldiers were just enough to whet their appetites for more. I constantly daydreamed about eating double portions of Wiener Schnitzel with fried eggs on top. And loads of fried potatoes, all in one of those small but cozy restaurants with wood paneling and red and white checkered table cloths. I wondered if such wonderful times would ever come back. However, we had plenty of fatless vegetables, potato soup and black bread mixed with wood shavings, according to rumors. Our uniforms and shoes were in bad shape, too. I had a cap made out of some sort of grass fiber. We never could win this war against such superiority, and I did not care much either. There was nothing I could do about it.

Our newspapers were full of gibberish about resisting to the last man unless the Allies could make decent peace proposals. But, by then it was very clear that our enemies could and would crush us. Through history, the German soldier has been known for his good fighting qualities. I do not know why. In peacetime, however, no people are more industrious or more peaceful. Fistfights or attacks with knives and pistols practically were unknown among grownups. I never saw a fight, except among school children.

Good news

On April 1, 1918, a messenger brought me a note signed by a full general:

Command of 23rd Reserve Corps
Headquarters April 1, 1918

In the name of his Majesty the Emperor and King I am decorating the Lieutenant of the Reserve Nagel of K Flak 82 with the Iron Cross 1. Class.

Signed
XXX
General of Infantry

At the same time I was told to go out for a few more days and then get ready for a transfer to a new artillery school for officers of the brand new 88 mm. anti-aircraft batteries. Nothing could suit me better and I eagerly waited for my orders to come through.

The men of K Flak 82 were the best soldiers I ever saw, and so easy to get along with. From now on I knew they would have a very hard time. On August 8, 1918, the Allies broke through in this sector, attacking with swarms of tanks, infantry and endless reserves. In his memoirs Ludendorff called this date the "Black Day." K Flak 82 was still operating in that area so I wrote and asked for news. A Lieutenant Hausherr (I did not know him) answered under the date of August 27, 1918. The guy still had not lost his sense of humor. He addressed his letter to me, calling me gustav nagel. At that time gustav nagel was a famous nut who walked naked all around Germany. He made speeches declaring that everything would be fine if people abandoned all capital letters and let their beards grow. His beard reached to the floor.

Lt. Hausherr wrote:

Thanks very much for your lines. Because you are still interested in us I will write you not over three lines: We are in a mess and a deep one. On the same road we advanced in spring we are now retreating, but slowly. During the first day when there was no field artillery here we had to join the fight of the songs and chariot on

the ground. They could not get sufficient ammo to us. Under those hardships motor and gun broke down every few minutes. At this moment all K Flaks and three heavy Flaks are kaput. The Tommies took away all the guns from Lt. Roth. Martin received the Iron Cross First Class. K Flak 82 is in bad shape. Heavy losses — eight men, our commander killed, non-coms Han, Loewert and gunner Fohman wounded, Petzold sick with dysentery. But what can we do? Personally, I am fine, but wish you could help us a little.

None of these names were familiar to me. The officer and men killed or wounded was bad news coming from an outfit consisting of only one officer and seven men to begin with. I wished I could find out what had happened to the crew I knew.

I took my time in getting to the artillery school in Lille. In Cambrai I had nice quarters and the next day I arrived in Lille where the school was located in the best part of town. For a few days we did nothing but wait for the school to open officially on April 6. Quarters were excellent. To me these training courses were like vacations. Some 150 officers were supposed to learn enough about this new 88 mm. gun so they could go out and take command after the course was completed.

The first evening we were fed in a large, barnlike hall. I did not know anybody. Most of the men were older and seemed to be of the reserve, with the exception of the colonel and his aides who were professionals.

These army dinners were always on the formal side. Nobody sat down until the colonel did and everybody was called by his rank with the prefix "Mister." The use of first names was out of the question.

The colonel introduced himself while all of us stood up. The dinner was supposed to begin, but the colonel asked for silence. He said he had received a telegram from Supreme Headquarters in Kreuznach, Germany, dated April 6, which he now wished to read with great pleasure. Of course, everybody thought peace had broken out. We could go home. How wonderful! But after hearing the telegram's first sentence, anybody could have knocked me down with a feather. I heard my name, but I became too confused to understand the rest:

During the storming of Albert, the Lt. Nagel of K Flak 82 rendered valuable services to the infantry by his resolute and successful action. Shooting down an enemy infantry flier on the same morning added more success to the Flak. To the Lt. Nagel and his crew of K Flak 82 I convey my full appreciation for his courageous conduct and his fine performance.

The Commanding General
von Hoeppner

After the reading there was complete silence. The colonel spoke: "If this Lt. Nagel is present, will he please come forward to receive this telegram?" He handed it to me with the remark that I was the first Flak officer so honored. There was a lot of handshaking and noise. The rest of the evening passed in a general celebration. It was very pleasant for me and I liked it, but I felt more like a freak of some sort than anything else.

Every two weeks the High Command published a short, army-type newspaper under the title "Special Deeds." Our action in the battle for Albert received a generous amount of publicity and in one issue we shared some of the glory with the exploits of the fliers and submarines. I had a copy but lost it.

A new weapon

For the first time I met the second lieutenant commanding my new outfit — heavy K Flak battery Nr. 179. Lt. Braus was a dealer in lumber in private life. He was about 40 years old, very friendly and easy to get along with. Lt. Braus obviously loved the good life and I wondered how we would find enough food to keep his big stomach well filled.

Our training course took three weeks and was quite pleasant. The new 88 mm. gun carried a considerably more powerful punch than the 77 mm. gun. Now we could engage enemy fliers much earlier while they were still far away from their targets. We had two guns, each drawn by a tractor that was equipped with a steel rope to pull the gun out of any ditch or deep mud. But our most prized possession was a small, two-seater type of open sports car for the use of Lt. Braus and myself.

Lille was only about eight miles behind the front lines and close to the Belgian-French border. My diary mentions frequent bombings. One day, just as Lt. Braus and I were leaving our comfortable quarters, a bomb or shell hit two elderly civilians and one of our soldiers. The civilians were killed, while we dragged the wounded man into the door of our quarters. The next day a bomb hit a childrens' school while in session. Everybody ran there to help. I did not go for fear the sight of bombed children would make me sick.

The destructive power of bombs seemed to increase all the time. A British Handley Page bomber used bombs of 1,000 kilos. Bombs of 300 kilos were in daily use. Even the small 50-kilo bombs had a destructive power equal to a 15 cm. shell, and anybody who had survived a nearby explosion of a 15 cm. shell would testify that such a shell could do fearful damage. All these missiles had to be feared. A 12½-kilo bomb dropped on living targets moving on hard ground would burst into 1,400 pieces, each one sizzling parallel to the ground, and could cause very bad wounds.

By this time, enemy tank tactics also were well developed and much feared, especially because the German army had missed the boat — we had only a few. Only artillery could hope to cope with this menace, and we had special instructions as to how our 88 mm. guns should be used against tanks. Tanks advanced in front of enemy infantry, firing their machine-guns and cannons. They had a speed of only four miles per hour but were able to overrun infantry with ease, unless the troops were supported by plenty of well trained field artillery or K Flak. However, there was not enough artillery on our side to successfully fight the swarms of tanks now appearing on the battlefields. In attacking a field artillery battery, the tanks would spread out and finally attack from the rear, mowing down the gun crews with their cannons and machine-guns. We had no good defense against it.

On May 2, 1918, the guns and equipment were turned over to us. The next day we were shipped on flatcars to Valenciennes to protect an army headquarters. We barely were in position when seven De Havilland bombers attacked the town. I thought our shooting was very poor. Many members of the crew were elderly men which made me think we were scraping the bottom of the barrel. They were too slow and by the time they executed the commands, the bombers were miles away. The next day five De Havillands came back and our shooting was better. We scattered the formation. On May 29, we had a substantial night attack by bombers, but the searchlight crew never managed to hold the targets long enough for us to take our measurements and observe the explosions.

Suddenly, on June 8, we were loaded on flatcars again and had no idea of our destination. We asked the train personnel, but they were under orders not to tell. We went through Luxembourg and after three days of travel we unloaded at Metz on the Mosel River. Metz was one of the strongest German fortresses, built as a counter measure to the French fortress at Verdun, 35 miles due west. Metz was about seven to 10 miles behind the St. Mihiel front now held by the newly arrived American army under General Pershing.

This front had been quiet for several years because, from a strategic point of view, it offered no prospects to either side, although it was a suitable training ground for inexperienced troops. The arrival of American soldiers enabled French soldiers to be thrown into the battles now raging further north along the Western Front.

It was quite difficult for me to grasp the fact that the soldiers opposing us were Americans, willing and eager to fight. All of my father's overseas friends were Americans. They had come to our house often and were outgoing, friendly types. From my earliest childhood I remember one who was a tobacco man from Virginia. He came every year, bringing with him a barrel of delicious Virginia apples for us.

In addition, my brother was an American citizen. When he arrived in the United States in 1908 he was a trained soldier of the 23rd Field Artillery Regiment, stationed in Coblenz. Now he was an American. When the United States entered the war in April 1917, it needed all the trained soldiers it could get. I was sure they had drafted him and that he probably was right in front of us among the 1,000,000 American soldiers now on French soil. We had not heard from him for more than a year. All this disturbed me very much. That we now had to face all these American soldiers was proof to me that our diplomats must have been the worst in the world. It was unbelievable.

After the American declaration of war, I had many discussions with my family as to the importance of it. When young, my father was rejected for some physical defect and did not have to serve in the army. Things military did not interest him at all. He had been in Kentucky and Virginia several times and in his opinion, Americans would make poor soldiers because they were unable to subject themselves to rigid discipline. Apart from this, many German people who had lifelong dealings with Americans felt vaguely that they simply would not fight us, even if their government told them to do so. This feeling was based on the fact that we seemed to have no grounds for a quarrel. Yes, American citizens had lost their lives on the Lusitania, but why did they choose to travel on a British liner carrying ammunition? And President Wilson's pronouncements concerning democracy and liberty touched a subject rather strange and unfamiliar to even the most educated German. The German people were quite content with their form of government. Furthermore, so my father thought, America had no army to speak of and there was nothing in its history to suggest a military mind. I could not agree with this viewpoint and when I read to my family some data concerning the American Civil War, they were astonished to find that both sides had lost more men than Germany had fighting in the Franco-German war. The Union and Confederacy fought each other with the utmost tenacity for four years. Yes, but they have no skill, they said. To this I could only answer that 85 percent of their soldiers were of Anglo-Saxon or German extraction. They had been training for more than a year now and would be just as good as the Germans and British were when the war started in 1914. And soldiers on both sides then were good enough to kill each other wholesale.

Protecting Metz

The country around Metz looks somewhat like the low hills of Pennsylvania. Metz was surrounded by forts, all of them on hills. Our battery was stationed on top of one of these hills, from where we could see into the valley of the Mosel River for miles. It was very pretty country. Since the arrival of the American army, Metz had become an important depot which needed protection from constantly increasing air attacks. The civilian population had not been evacuated and life went on more or less in normal fashion. Enemy bombers concentrated on the areas around the railway station where all of the depots were located.

As far as military activities were concerned, for us it was a war deluxe. The forts were constructed of concrete and earth 15 feet thick — immune to the heaviest artillery fire known. Deep inside were our quarters, warm and comfortable with beds, chairs and tables. I had one huge room all to myself with a window looking out on the beautiful Mosel Valley.

The six or seven anti-aircraft batteries stationed on the surrounding hills were under the command of Captain of the Reserve Soll, an overaged professor of math from some university. He was very polite and precise and had worked out all kinds of formulas for the destruction of the bombers coming over regularly in good flying weather. But none of them worked. I cannot remember a single bomber coming down.

The June weather was beautiful. Our battery commander, Lt. Braus, loved good wine and a few yards from the guns the crew handbuilt a sort of pergola where we could while away the summer days. Lt. Braus had had little war experience so far and he apparently enjoyed trying his shooting skill. But with all the batteries shooting at the same time, it was impossible to trace our shots. I did very little firing and was glad Lt. Braus took over most of that duty. He often mixed a fine drink for us consisting of Mosel wine, fizzy water and fresh peaches, perforated with a fork. We drank it under our precious pergola that was erected in the midst of flower beds planted by the crew. It was a most comfortable life.

My diary says that on June 12, 1918, a squadron of five bombers came over, dropped bombs close to the depot and flew away unharmed. Lt. Braus shot 65 rounds. After each raid Captain Soll would hold endless conversation with each battery, explaining why we did not hit anything. The next time we were ordered to aim not at the fliers, but to put a concentrated fire over the depots.

At the first meeting I noticed that most of the battery commanders were overaged officers, while their deputies were younger ones of my age, evidently sent here for a rest.

Metz was ranked as a first-class fortress. In peacetime it had 61,000 inhabitants, of which 25,000 were soldiers. France had to surrender the fortress after the war of 1870-71, and quite a number of the inhabitants only spoke French when I was there. The streets were narrow and crooked, dominated by the large cathedral built in the 13th century.

Whenever bombers made a raid they always hit something and seeing part of Metz burning was a common sight, exciting no one. The town had nothing to offer for amusement and I never went down to look at the bomb damage. Restaurants would not serve their bad meals without a ration card. During the summer the heat was intense and never again did I see a town so dusty and full of flies. We had no reason to leave our comfortable hill.

June 23 was a lively day. Several bomber squadrons came over and we shot 120 rounds. Later on the sky became cloudy and we hoped for a peaceful night. But from midnight until 3 a.m., they came back. The searchlight crews had trouble holding the targets and we seemed to do no good at all. Large fires started burning in Metz. One big Handley Page circled our battery at leisure and Lt. Braus seemed to have a good time banging away. I watched from our pergola, sipping some more of his latest mixture. All this warlike activity seemed perfectly harmless to me and I wondered why my wife could not simply buy a railroad ticket and visit me. Metz still was full of civilians and they paid little attention to the bombing. What difference would one more civilian make anyway? But I found out that the commanding general of the Metz garrison first had to give his permission. To my astonishment, permission was granted promptly, but I began worrying about the safety measures.

To let her live in a hotel downtown was much too dangerous. She would be safest with me on the fort. No enemy plane ever attempted to attack us with bombs or machine-guns. While we were shooting she could go down into the fort where she would be perfectly safe. But how could I get her to the fort? I did not want to ask Captain Soll. He was the cautious type and certainly would say "No". However, he came regularly for inspections in his car which did not have rubber tires — only ordinary wagon wheels — and they made quite a racket while coming up the rather steep hill. That would give me plenty of warning. I did not know what orders or regulations I was breaking by bringing her up to the fort, but I considered it a very slight risk. Captain Soll had no standing as a soldier and if he would accuse me of a serious offense I was sure my "friend" General von Hoeppner would laugh it off. Of course, I had to tell the crew and they were very enthusiastic about it.

There was only one train and it arrived at night at irregular hours to avoid being bombed. It would arrive anytime between midnight and early morning, carrying passengers and everything else needed to supply the armies in front of Metz. Losses caused by bombings were kept as secret as possible, but it became known that one bomb once hit the diner filled with soldiers. In case of enemy action, we had to get my wife off the railroad platform and down the steps quickly, load her into a truck and then step on the gas. We decided to equip our closed truck with a sofa, blanket, medicine and bandages. Next to the sofa Lt. Braus had placed a bucket with ice and a bottle of champagne. To be prepared for everything I showed my wife's picture to the men and they knew they had to bring her out dead or alive.

On July 3 at 3 a.m., the train finally came puffing in. It was a cloudy night and nothing happened. Our welcoming committee, consisting of two officers, one top sergeant, one chauffeur and four men, quickly lifted Dorothy into the truck. Before Lt. Braus introduced himself he made her drink some champagne and off we rolled. It had been a strenuous trip for her. The train was filled with soldiers and stopped very often for no apparent reasons. One woman passenger was going to Metz to attend the funeral of a sister killed by a bomb. Another woman seemed to be drunk and her stories were not comforting. But now the trip was over. Inside the truck we were quite a crowd and everybody was quite amused by her travel adventures.

For the first few days I quartered her in a very primitive rooming house. We went for long walks despite the heat, flies and dust. The front lines were not far away. Captive balloons — many of them — were clearly visible. To see a flaming balloon come down was quite an adventure for Dorothy. During our walks we often saw attacking bombers coming over in formation. Once we were bathing our feet in the cool Mosel River on a very hot day about a mile outside of town, when all of the Flak batteries opened up. Bombers came flying right over our heads. It was a fascinating spectacle which we watched in comfort and without thought of danger. Suddenly I heard some big pieces of shells coming down and land with a thud close by. We threw ourselves to the ground, but I was frightened. What a silly situation to be in. It could have been bad. These splinters from our own shells must have done considerable damage, but I never heard of anybody being killed by them.

Trouble started when Lt. Braus obtained a two-week leave. Now I had to stay at the fort day and night, so I took Dorothy with me. My men became quite fond of her and did all they could to make her comfortable. They even strung an extra telephone line to our living quarters in the fort so they could warn us whenever Captain Soll's car puffed up the hill. It worked very well. One day the good captain came into quarters while Dorothy was hiding in the closet. This really was a silly thing to do. Had he discovered her, it would have been difficult to introduce her as my wife. While she lived on the fort we had the usual alarms and shootings. I delegated one soldier to stay with her downstairs, but I did not realize that the firing of our 88 mm. gun overhead made an almost unbearable noise, echoing with tremendous force through the concrete roof and walls. It frightened her at first. Soon another crisis arose. Our battery was ordered to take position on another hill fort a few miles closer to the front. I was told to identify myself to the infantry sentries at the bottom of the hill.

I knew these sentries would never let a woman through and I had the feeling something drastic had to be done this time to keep Dorothy with me. My men were very loyal to me and I knew they would not blabber about it. All of them thought the whole thing would be a big lark and a good time would be had by all. By now Dorothy had become a sort of battery mascot, and we were not giving her up that easily. So, I gave her my officer's overcoat and cap. She stuffed her hair carefully inside. As we approached the sentries we had to stop for routine identification. The sentry looked at the driver and then saw two "officers," one apparently sleeping with "his" head down. The sentry promptly waved us on. This time I had to take a bigger chance. The sentries at the foot of the hill clearly indicated that no civilians and no women would be allowed to enter this fort.

On August 8 Dorothy's visiting permit expired and she had to leave.

Outgoing trucks were not inspected and we had no trouble, but I could not bring her to the depot because Lt. Braus had not yet returned from his leave. Her train departed just before sunrise without enemy interference.

The Americans attack

A week or so later the enemy increased his bombings. On August 15 our gun positions were bombed for the first and only time. All three bombs landed on the slopes of our hill without doing damage. That day we fired 120 rounds — and so it went in routine fashion until September 12, when the new American army mounted its first major attack in the St. Mihiel sector, seven to 10 miles in front of our position. Before describing this action, let me give some information about the overall situation on the Western Front.

The German armies were in very bad shape. Every soldier and civilian was hungry. Losses in material could not be replaced and the soldiers arriving as replacements were too young, poorly trained and often unwilling to risk their necks because the war now looked like a lost cause. Since the Allied breakthrough on August 8 in the Albert-Moreuil sector, the enemy's superiority in men and guns became visible to even the simplest soldier, and morale was breaking down gradually. On that same day, August 8, seven German divisions were routed by a fierce tank attack, and for the first time the German High Command realized the German soldier could not hold out much longer. Peace feelers were sent out with the help of the Swedish and Swiss governments, but the Allies knew that Germany was beaten and therefore were in no mood for talks. And now a brand new and large American army was ready to attack.

A few days before, I had seen about 20 American soldiers who had been taken prisoner and were marching by to be shipped to some prison camp. They looked healthy, well-fed and above everything else, their marvelous clothing and uniform accessories impressed us. Everything they had seemed to be of the best — fine heavy boots and thick and solid leather for their gun holsters, belts and gloves. All of them were chewing furiously, which confounded the bystanders until I explained to them the importance of chewing gum to the American way of life. Most Germans never had heard of chewing gum. I never had seen chewing gum myself, but I knew about it.

General Pershing was anxious to test his army. He ordered it to straighten out and eliminate the German lines jutting into the sector like a long finger 25 miles deep and about 10 miles wide in the middle. It took too many German troops to hold the 25-mile long sides. When these troops were packing up to retreat, the American attack near St. Mihiel surprised them. American troops pierced both sides and orders were given to the Germans to manage a fighting retreat.

From our hill we clearly could see that something fairly big was going on. Exploding shells in great quantities were everywhere and all hell suddenly seemed to break loose. Although we were only some seven miles behind the battlefield, it was impossible to guess how the battle was going. Nobody in Metz appeared to be alarmed. But while all this was happening, every window in the town and in our fort rattled more than I had ever heard before. A few broke. General Pershing succeeded and when it was all over, the front line was straight.

On the second day of the St. Mihiel battle, September 13, a neighboring Flak shot down a bomber after it had done great damage, coming in at 100 yards. About half the town seemed to be in flames.

For the first time very heavy American shells exploded close to our fort. They were aiming at the Mosel River bridge at the foot of our hill. The next day, September 14, swarms of bombers came over in waves and we fired all day long and part of the night.

On September 17 we heard that our allies, the Austrians, were suing for peace. The end seemed near. Our army High Command wanted to hold out and fight, hoping our enemies might find the going too costly. Personally, I had no strong feelings about victory or defeat. I had read enough to know that the river of history never ceases in its flow and that its course is capricious, meandering and quite unpredictable. I was sure we had lost the war, but with the exception of a small strip of East Prussia, no enemy had crossed the German border. The German people had suffered much less than the French, Belgians and Russians, on whose territories the battles were fought. I could not see much advantage in being the victor. Each individual and all of the soldiers fighting each other at this moment somehow would still have to make a living and build up their own lives, winner and loser alike. Those were the thoughts I jotted down in my diary at that time.

On September 22 the commanding general defending Metz praised the Flak for the first time, saying they had shot down 12 bombers. That astonished me. It must have happened while I was sleeping or paying no attention. I did not personally see a single plane come down.

On October 13 we heard about President Wilson's famous 14 Points which had to be accepted before peace negotiations could start. Nobody in our outfit seemed to be interested in these fine points of international diplomacy. We lost the war. Let's finish it the best we can and go home. In short, I saw nothing catastrophic in losing this war. It happened before in history. Nations and people always survived.

I thought I would end the war here at the fort, although I could not quite picture the end. If the victorious Allies intended to enter Germany without granting an armistice, they first would have to conquer Metz, and in that case, we would have to stand and fight once more. But what could we do? Our guns could not be lowered enough to fire down the hill and would be more or less useless. We had two machine-guns. To some staff officer it might look on paper that two 88 mm. guns and two machine-guns could hold a hill for a long time. But in reality, we were helpless if infantry should come up the hill of ours. As far as I knew, nobody had any worthwhile experience in firing machine-guns.

Without previous warning, I received orders on October 30 to report the next day to the commander of heavy K Flak Battery Nr. 112, stationed near the little town of Gorz. Gorz was seven or eight miles in front of Metz where our lines had stabilized after the St. Mihiel battle. To leave this comfortable assignment and once more join a front line outfit came as a bad surprise.

Before joining K Flak 112, I reported to the group commander of that district. He was not there but his aide enlightened me plenty. He expressed his regret that I had to join this battery, but the second- in-command, a lieutenant, was sick. He then went on to say I would have a very hard time because the captain of the reserve commanding the battery was an impossible person to get along with. According to the aide, this captain was incompetent, a liar, a coward and hated by his men, and nobody could understand why a man of such character had been promoted to officer rank in the first place. But, so he said, I should defend myself and not give in to him. It was a queer conversation. This man gave me to understand that in case of serious trouble between the captain and myself, the group commander would take my word and not his. I expected all kinds of difficulties. But the commander of K Flak 112 — I have forgotten his name — seemed to have no standing whatever with his superior. If he ordered me to do some foolish thing, I would refuse. I felt quite confident.

When I reported to the battery the next day, the captain looked harmless enough — a small, squatty man on the fat side. I noticed he had no battlefield decorations of any kind and I could not help wondering what he had done all this time. He received me in very friendly fashion and said he knew my name from dispatches published in the army newspapers. It was time for some sort of supper when I arrived and he apologized that he already had eaten. However, he had saved something for me. In came the most wonderful supper I had seen for a long time: one whole partridge, cabbage, a potato and red wine. That fellow greatly rose in my estimation, for at least he had a talent obtaining good food. I thanked him; he opened up another bottle of wine and began explaining the local situation, which seemed to be desperate.

Facing us was a huge American army of fresh troops which had not participated in the last St. Mihiel battle. They were anxious to prove their worth on the battlefield. Intelligence reported increased preparations every day for a large attack in our sector. American superiority in guns was estimated at 17 to one, with supplies of unlimited ammunition. Our worn out infantry in front of us would be overrun quickly and engulfed in a sea of fresh and excellently equipped soldiers from the United States.

Our guns were in position in a forest surrounding us on all sides, and enemy soldiers coming out of these woods could shoot us up with the greatest of ease. Because the trees were so close we could only shoot upwards. This would be satisfactory as long as we could function as an anti-aircraft battery. We were apprehensive and wondered if the Americans would get us before the war would end.

On November 7 I had my only disagreement with the captain. A lone artillery spotting plane came over our position at dusk, a time that was best for spotting artillery flashes. Our gun positions were well camouflaged with branches and nettings and I had ordered the men not to move around while the spotter plane was nearby. At that time the captain was about 500 yards behind in our quarters and, of course, had seen the plane. He phoned and ordered me to open up and shoot the plane down. This was a very foolish order under the circumstances and I argued with him at length. The conversation became a little heated and I flatly refused, calling the idea just plain stupid. Now he began to irritate me. He hung up and I did not shoot. He himself had told me the American superiority in guns was overwhelming. Had we fired, the spotter plane would have radioed our position within seconds and we would have been buried under an avalanche of heavy shells. It would have been suicide. We would have been blasted off the map.

The end

On November 8 we heard a revolution had broken out in Germany. It had started in the navy. Since the battle of Jutland, fought in May 1916, the officers in the German battle fleet considered themselves superior in skill and seamanship to the British navy. The prospect of being forced to surrender their proud ships because the army was collapsing seemed completely unacceptable to them. The battle of Jutland was the only full scale sea battle of the war, with both sides appearing in full strength and clashing in the North Sea, although the German fleet was outnumbered three to two. Because night came this battle was not fought to the finish. The British losses in ships and men were greater than those on the German side. Among our navy's losses was the battleship "Posen," commanded by the brother-in-law of Lt. Schroeder who had been my commanding officer for most of my time in Russia. I still remember when the telegram announcing his brother-in-law's death arrived while we were eating.

Now, when the end was in sight, the German naval officers intended to go out and go down fighting. When orders were given to the stokers to fire up the boilers, they refused. The crews were quite unwilling to sacrifice their lives in this useless gesture. For the first time in German history, seamen refused to obey their officers and fights broke out on several ships. Some captains were killed in the following confusion. The revolution was on, spreading very quickly to the army. The whole might of the German armed forces collapsed almost overnight. Suddenly, men who had been disciplined soldiers and seamen became an unruly and dangerous mob armed to the teeth, and were willing to murder anybody resisting them. For the orderly mass of German soldiers, all this was shocking and dangerous. Should we now fight these revolutionaries and start a civil war? Nobody seemed to know and there was no overall leadership. The Kaiser fled to Hollard and General Ludendorff, the chief of staff, had fled to Sweden. Everyone for himself seemed to be the motto. That was the situation on November 11, 1918, when the armistice was declared. What worried me most was the terrible news reaching us from home. Drunken soldiers roamed the streets. Even the police were reported to have joined the revolution. Some of these reports were exaggerated, but we did not know it then. The people at home were terrified.

At this time, while all discipline apparently had collapsed, socalled "Soviet Soldiers' and Navy Councils" were formed under the leadership of the worst elements. One of their main objects seemed to be getting rid of those officers they hated.

As the battery captain and I were sitting down to dinner on one of the last nights, he found an alarming message on the table. I cannot remember for sure, but I believe the message was wrapped around a stone and thrown into our room. The message ordered the captain to leave the battery immediately. If he refused, he was threatened to be killed by a hand grenade. He lost his composure and, stripped of his power by the events, he was not much of a man. He begged me to drive him to the nearest railroad station right away. I did, driving the little passenger car belonging to the battery. Next to me was a member of the local Soviet Soldiers' Council, whose red armband served as a sort of passport. Fearing recognition as an officer, the captain had torn off his insignia and made himself very small in the back seat. The trip was uneventful. But what next?

I had been with this battery only 10 days and did not know who the troublemakers were, nor did I wish to find out why they seemed to hate their captain. That might lead to arguments and would help no one. When we returned, the men of the battery attended one of the soldiers' council meetings. Being quite curious I entered the hall and listened to what was going on. Conditions of the armistice gradually became known. We had to give up territory and retreat every day for so many miles. I believe it was 10 miles per day. Stragglers would be taken prisoner by the American army, following us a few miles behind. I must say that the men of that revolutionary council treated me with respect and after a long palaver, asked me if I would lead them home. They realized we would obtain food and gas only if we marched as a unit. They promised to obey and did so. In this outfit, discipline never broke down after the men had eliminated their captain. Until the very last day we marched together. They addressed me in the third person and attended to the military courtesies as was customary in the German army. I had no difficulties of any kind.

All K Flak batteries in our sector decided to march together — 10 officers and 193 men. The march home ordinarily would have been a depressing affair. The weather was cold and rainy. The population knew that its territory between the French-German border and the Rhine River would be occupied by American and French armies marching a few miles behind us. Inspite of this the people were cheerful and did their best for us. Some towns and villages had erected welcome signs across the roads. But the tremendous joy and relief that the war finally had come to an end dominated our emotions completely. Whatever awaited us from now on in civilian life would be easy by comparison. I was not at all afraid of the future. It would be a very nice life, I was sure of it.

It took us eight days to reach the Rhine. We always had good, warm quarters and most of the time the people with whom we were quartered invited me to eat supper with them. Often, they asked me what had caused the revolt in the army. Why had discipline collapsed all of a sudden, without warning?

To begin with, it must be said that not all of the army was in revolt. Most of the men simply wanted to get home. They had no ambitions as revolutionaries whatever. There was no political leadership anyway; it simply was a revolt against authority by a small part of the army. For more than four years strict discipline had been enforced. Men and officers, some of them four-times wounded, had to be sent back into the front lines. Some regiments were thrown into battle time after time while others occupied quiet fronts. It was impossible to distribute the burdens and dangers of combat fairly; so much of it was due to good or bad luck. When the news reached the army that some navy men successfully had defied their officers for the first time in history, and had even killed some without being shot themselves, some of the simple-minded soldiers in the army thought a new, wonderful way of life had arrived. But before they could exploit this new life fully, they had to get rid of their officers, and after they had chased them away or had killed them, all the pleasures of a full life would be theirs. From now on they would be on top, so they thought. My opinion always has been that only a small proportion of the army had gone berserk.

Too many hardships and too much suffering temporarily had transformed some German soldiers into stupid and dangerous crackpots. Nothing could be gained by a revolution. The German government as we knew it during our lifetime already had been swept away by events. Imperial Germany did not exist anymore, so, what or whom did they want to overthrow? There was no sensible answer. I felt this trouble would pass. Still, it worried me to be surrounded by thousands of soldiers — most of them obeying orders and behaving well — but some in a state of revolt against all authority and heavily armed with rifles and hand grenades. I had not carried a revolver since I was promoted to officer rank because sidearms handicapped movements and I thought them useless. But now, we all carried sidearms to protect ourselves from drunken, marauding soldiers who might appear at any time. The overall situation was lawless and we worried about what might be going on in our hometowns. Rumor had it that some good and loyal divisions already were fighting inside Germany to restore order.

On November 22 we reached the Rhine bridge near Kaiserslautern. Dirty and sloppy looking revolutionary soldiers wearing red armbands stopped us and refused to let us cross the bridge. They feared our cannons as well as the thought that our whole outfit would join the counter-revolutionary army rumored to be forming beyond the Rhine, out of reach of the French-American armies that would stop at the river, according to the armistice conditions. So I palavered with them a little. They were quite orderly and polite, but I really did not care what happened to the guns. According to the armistice conditions, the guns were to be surrendered and turned over officially to the French or American armistice commissions at some assembly point anyway. I agreed to let these men have the guns against proper receipt for two motorized Flak guns, two trucks and one passenger automobile. After these formalities were over, we parked the vehicles on the west side of the Rhine and then proceeded on foot to the other side of the bridge. I shook hands with every man and dismissed them with instructions to get home the best way they could. That was the end of the war for me.

A light K-Flak in position for firing.

A retouched photo postcard showing a light K-Flak supporting infantry. Note combat positions of the officer and gun crew.

Members of K-Flak 82, February 1918. Chauffeur Rupp sits at upper left.

K-Flak 82's camouflaged gun in position near Honnecourt-Franqueville, March 1918.

Abandoned British artillery wagons in front of Albert, March 1918.

British tank destroyed by German K-Flak battery near Albert, March 1918.

Nagel, April 1918. The photo was taken in Lille shortly after he received the Iron Cross first class.

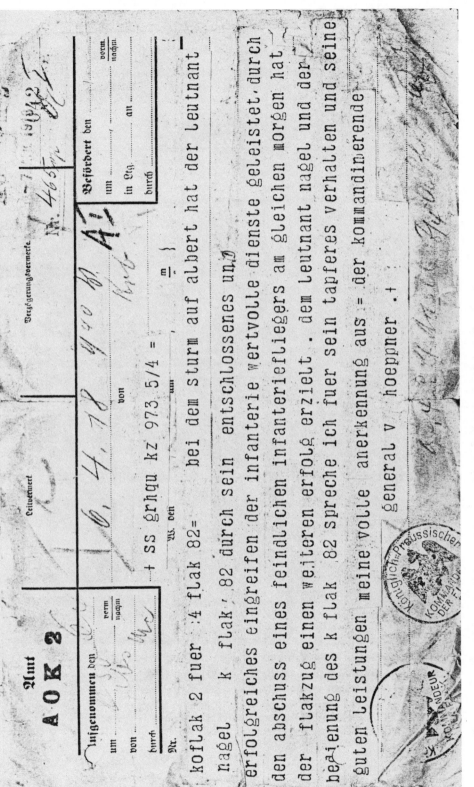

Congratulatory message to Nagel from General von Hoeppner, commander of the German Air Service.

An 88 mm. heavy K-Flak gun (not Nagel's) painted in mottled camouflage colors. This gun weighed some 6,700 pounds and fired a shell weighing 21 pounds. The barrel could be elevated to 70 degrees, muzzle velocity was about 2,600 feet per second and vertical range was 12,600 feet.

Feldwebel Grueterich (left) and Leutnant Braus in K-Flak 179's passenger car on the train from Lille to Metz, June 8, 1918.

K-Flak 179 moving into position on the East Fort outside Metz, June 1918.

Enlisted crew of K-Flak 179 atop the East Fort, Metz, August 1918.

Wearing Nagel's cap and overcoat, Dorothy poses in the disguise used to sneak her past German sentries, Metz, July 1918.

Dorothy loading K-Flak 179's 88 mm. gun on the East Fort, Metz, July 1918.

Dorothy and Fritz 'team up' on a heavy Maxim machine-gun, Metz, July 1918.

Fritz and Dorothy

SEVEN

1919-1921

Hard times at home

My last report to K Flak headquarters in Hannover, which included the receipts for the guns, must never have reached there. For several months they asked me all kinds of questions as to the whereabouts of the guns, trucks and auto. Finally, I refused to answer and the matter went to sleep.

I reached Bremen on November 24, 1918, and soon noticed my nervous system did not seem to function right. While in the army I never had trouble sleeping whenever I had the opportunity, but now at home, I could not sleep. I felt weak and had horrible nightmares. I forgot how long it took me to straighten out, but it was some time.

My family had survived fairly well. My father had lost a lot of weight. At the outbreak of the war he had quite a stomach sticking out; now he was a thin man. My mother was not as thin but had lost heavily, too. My wife had had no fat to lose, but the shortage of food, especially the almost complete lack of fat, had created physical and nervous disorders. The doctor said only a sufficient intake of solid food could cure her ailments.

At home in Bremen the local situation was bad. The Allies kept the blockade on to force Germany to sign the peace treaty they now were working out among themselves. Therefore, Germany could not import food and had to rely on its own resources for many months to come. The final peace treaty was signed on June 28, 1919, and even then, imports of food by a bankrupt Germany were slow in coming in.

In the meantime, everybody did their best to find food for their families. There still was no overall German authority managing fair distribution of available food. In Bremen, city authorities did the best they could trying to convince nearby farmers to deliver food to the Bremen market. But inflation had set in and soon the farmers sold their produce at whatever the traffic could bear. Only people with money could pay these prices. What kept us going in reasonable comfort was my mother-in-law's pension. It amounted to 300 pounds sterling per year — about $1,400 — a large sum of money in inflation-ridden Germany at that time. Pounds sterling were equal to gold. The worse the inflation, the more marks we would obtain when changing the sterling into marks. But the food we craved — butter, sugar, good flour and meat — could not be bought at any price because the farmers refused to sell.

On top of these difficulties the lawless elements became more numerous and more dangerous. Break-ins of the homes of the wealthy were common. Prominent citizens were abducted and held for ransom. Workers' strikes were going on almost daily. I especially remember a strike by the workers of the waterworks. What they wanted I cannot remember, but we had no drinking water, no toilet would flush and nothing could be washed. Water had to be dipped from the small lakes in a nearby park, out of the Weser River or from anywhere it could be found. When that happened the better elements managed a strike of their own to teach the strikers that we were not helpless. As a countermeasure, all activities ceased. No doctor would make house calls, no telephone would be answered and all stores, offices and banks were closed tight. Everybody simply refused to move or do anything. The town went dead. This counter strike hit the striking water men and their families hard. After about 10 days it was all over. A dangerous rift had developed between the common working man and the educated part of the population. Some sort of explosion, perhaps a bloody one, was possible. The local police were not effective or numerous enough; nobody knew for sure which side they were on anyway. We were uneasy. A new revolution like the French one in 1792 with all its terrors might break out. Who would or could protect the average law-abiding citizen?

One day I received a phone call telling me that all army or navy officers and all citizens able and willing to carry a rifle should meet in a nearby school. When this meeting was over I had joined the Bremen Stadtwehr, or City Defense Force, together with many other soldiers and civilians. We agreed to patrol all streets day and night, every day. A patrol consisted mostly of one man with war experience and one civilian, but always two men marching together. It was arranged for each patrol to protect its own city district as much as possible.

Fortunately, my parents' house and the flat where I lived with my wife and mother-in-law belonged to my patrol territory. My civilian partners were often engineers of the famous Vulcan shipbuilding firm, where many of our submarines had been constructed. Now the firm was idle. Every man was armed with a loaded rifle and each agreed to show up for patrol once a week, or more in emergencies, without pay. Patrol duty lasted one day and one night every week. The overall commander gave us authority to shoot or arrest when forced to do so, although he obviously had no legal right to commission this little private army. It was an emergency measure to protect our homes and families from marauding armed gangs. After we went into action, the citizens breathed easier. We had no trouble whatever in my district. But to patrol the streets for two hours at a time in bitter cold on a snowy night was no fun. Yet, nobody complained. It seemed as if our city defense forces had restored almost normal peace and tranquility when, in the beginning of February 1919, alarming news reached us.

In the country outside town several thousand men calling themselves "Spartacus" were assembling. Consisting mostly of the worst revolutionary elements of the now-dissolved army and navy, they were armed with rifles and some machine-guns for the purpose of taking the city of Bremen by force. If they succeeded the worst could be expected. These men were tough and not afraid to fight. According to rumors, many already had infiltrated into key points of the city and their machine-guns were in position to dominate the main streets.

Our private army was not strong enough or organized for large-scale fighting. Inside town the situation was tense. It was dangerous to use the telephone in connection with defense measures. Orders to the members of our force had to be given by word of mouth or over the phone by code. At the same time, intentionally of course, another big strike broke out again and nobody worked. We had no lights or water. Everybody was waiting for the attack.

When the first alarming reports came in from the country, the high command of our private army sent secret messengers to a loyal and orderly brigade of navy men which was in camp in some villages 15 miles away. There were several such outfits in existence in Germany. These men and their officers had no jobs awaiting them, and by sticking together they hoped to last long enough to be incorporated into some sort of police force which surely would be formed sooner or later. When our messengers had informed them fully, they were ready to move at once and fight for law and order. They had no artillery, but they did have some mortars and plenty of rifles and ammunition. A plan was worked out by which our city defense force would let the Spartacus men enter certain parts of the city, and when they had reached the main street leading to the Weser River bridge, our force would attack them. Meanwhile, the navy brigade of some 2,000 men would swarm over the bridge and mop them up from the rear, killing as many as they could.

The Spartacus men entered Bremen the morning of February 12 while our men offered light resistance. The citizens were terrified. A fight in the narrow streets could not lead to the annihilation of the enemy. They had to be drawn into the broad Kaiserstrasse leading to the bridge. That maneuver was quite successful, but at the last minute, two hours after the attack had started, a hitch developed. Our friends the navy men could not come across the bridge because unknown to us, a well-protected machine-gun had been placed by the Spartacists on top of the bridge, with another one on the roof of a tobacco warehouse. Luckily, we had a small armored car with a machine-gun. One of the crew members was a member of my tennis club. When this car rumbled forward to take up the fight with the enemy machine-guns, a Spartacus man with a white flag appeared, apparently wanting to talk to the men in the armored car. As they stepped out of their vehicle, they were shot down and killed, riddled with bullets. It happened in full sight and everybody saw it. Thereafter, the navy men swarmed over the bridge and the city forces could not be stopped either. How many Spartacus men were killed in the following massacre, nobody knew. Very few prisoners were taken and what happened to them also is unknown. Later on some newspapers accused our side of atrocities. This battle restored order and the Spartacus organization ceased to exist in Bremen. Eleven men were killed in our city defense force.

I had learned all this from my friends. I was not there because no one had given me orders. The day before the battle I had been on patrol duty. My partner and I had arrested one of the local Communist leaders, a screwball intellectual and portrait painter by profession whom I recognized although he tried to go through our roadblock camouflaged with a beard and dirty clothes. He offered no resistance. When I checked out to rest early the next morning, I was told I would be called in case the Spartacus fight started.

When I reached our flat the food situation was bad. My wife was pregnant and I had to get some decent food from somewhere. I climbed on my bicycle to visit some farmers with my pockets crammed full of money. I came back with some milk and a few eggs, but as I approached our street I saw, to my utter amazement, some 77 mm. shells screaming over our house and exploding close by. There was no fighting going on at all in our neighborhood. I knew our side had no guns, but how did the Spartacus people manage to have artillery? It seemed quite incomprehensible.

Bremen is a long, stretched-out city and I concluded the artillery had to be in a park just a few blocks from our flat. As I ran up the steps I found my family rather calm. One of the next shells exploded in a neighbor's garden and another slammed into nearby greenhouses belonging to my godfather, Karl Kommer. Shooting into private homes and gardens made no military sense at all. I never found out the reason, but I believe the Spartacus men manning this gun had no idea how to aim or handle it. They simply put in some shells, pulled the trigger and hoped they would kill somebody. Their sympathizers lived in a different district of town. But I was more frightened about my family than they were themselves and I was in no mood to leave them alone.

When it became known in the afternoon that the battle was over and won, people came out of their houses to thank their liberators. As we stood on the street to watch the proceedings, a group of navy men came by and halted to rest. We noticed they had some Spartacus prisoners. This excited the womenfolk and when Dorothy asked a navy man what would happen to these rather miserable-looking prisoners, he replied, grinning, "Oh, we will shoot them in a few minutes." I thought the man joked, but Dorothy and her mother took it seriously and hoped they would not do it right before their eyes. Nothing happened as far as I could see or hear.

After the military power of the Spartacus was broken, I was ordered to be a censor, along with an elderly civilian businessman. Our job was to read every incoming cable or telegram in cooperation with the postal authorities. Only messages inciting the people to revolution or civil disturbances were to be stopped from reaching their destinations. Every day we received long cables from a Russian revolutionary committee in Moscow, addressed to the Bremen "Workmen and Soldiers' Council," urging its members to continue the revolution. Each cable sounded like a lesson in Marxism, apparently intended for people who never had heard of Marxism before. "Religion is the opium of the people.....Production must be in the hands of the people.....Throw off your shackles.....etc., etc." None of the cables contained any worthwhile and specific instructions of how to reach these goals. They only were filled with phrases out of some textbook for Communists. The whole thing made no sense. Every day we threw these long-winded cables into the wastebasket without even reading them. In addition to these duties I tried to make some money, which was almost impossible while Germany was still blockaded.

Finally, in May and June of 1919, the final terms of surrender were handed to the Germans. This treaty of Versailles was a lengthy document which the German emissaries were forced to sign. The "Big Four" — Clemenceau of France, Lloyd George of Great Britain, Orlando of Italy and Wilson of the United States — had struggled among themselves for five months concerning the fate of Germany. It was now a republic under President Ebert, a man my father knew quite well. He was from Bremen where he had represented the working man in the city government, while my father represented the tobacco importers. Ebert was well respected and had been elected president of the German republic.

President Wilson had argued for a peace treaty that would permit the German people to exist. Wilson was not against reparations, but he and his advisers feared an excessively harsh and humiliating treaty would only lead to more bloodshed and revolt, and possibly to another war. The other three of the Big Four considered Wilson an idealistic fool who simply had no idea how a defeated enemy should be treated. Wilson's idea of a League of Nations was another impossible dream in the then prevailing atmosphere of hatred and revenge. When the American Congress even voted against Wilson and refused to have anything to do with the League of Nations or further European entanglements, Wilson's influence in European affairs came to an end. Now France and her allies had Germany at their mercy.

As most historians now agree, the conditions of the Treaty of Versailles simply could not be carried out. At first, things went fairly well. Germany surrendered whatever tangibles it possessed, such as what was left of gold, silver, the merchant fleet, colonies and everything that could be moved, including many thousands of cattle from the farmers' fields. But when it came to payments out of "profits," the impossibility of it all became apparent. The treaty said Germany must pay a "minimum" of 25 billion dollars in gold. How could such a sum be earned? The Allies intended to take all normal profits until Germany had paid all war costs. What would happen to the German people was of no interest to them. When payments of money ceased coming, the French army marched into the Ruhr, forcing the miners to work at bayonet point to mine coal to be shipped to France. They refused and fought the French with homemade weapons. The miners became heroes and were cheered, but the overall situation remained terribly insecure and nobody knew where the next meal would come from.

And so it went for quite a while. The government — the first republic established in Germany — had no power, no money and could do nothing to help the people. Germany's population, in the tradition of the desperate, was now ready to listen to anybody promising food, work and a normal life. We were a democracy, but everyday problems of existence seemed to get worse and people began doubting the efficiency of such a form of government. A strong man was wanted. Newspapers began talking about a man called Hitler, a paperhanger by profession, who had survived the war as a corporal. On the face of it he appeared to be some sort of uneducated crackpot, but the papers reported that thousands of people in Munich listened to his rantings every day. The rest is history and President Wilson's fears proved absolutely right.

A dream comes true

I became very anxious to leave Germany. My brother in America wrote that I should go to Rotterdam to see the American consul who already had instructions to visa my passport and permit all of my family to go to the United States. Our hopes rose. When I reached the consulate and told them what I wanted the atmosphere was very chilly. I was interviewed by a male assistant about my age. I never saw the consul. My explanations that I was a tobacco buyer and wanted to purchase tobacco for my father's firm, and that I had a brother who was an American citizen, seemed to interest no one. They wanted to know what I had done in the war and where I had been during the past four years. Maybe they thought I was a war criminal. When it was all over I was told the United States did not need and did not want people like me. Then another man gave me a lecture, explaining how much better the American soldiers were than the British, French and Germans, and so on. A complete fool, I thought. I returned to Bremen empty-handed. I explained this fiasco in a letter to my brother who promised to take up the matter with the State Department and Representative Barkley of Kentucky, who much later became vice-president of the United States.

I continued my services as a censor and patrolman in the city defense force, which was necessary because the mood of the people in sympathy with the Spartacus-Communist movement was ugly. Although their military organization had ceased to exist since the fight of February 12, 1919, the men of that group were still on hand and our enemies.

One day my wife and I went for a walk. Living on the edge of town we soon found ourselves somewhat lost amidst many small plots of land where people seemed to live in shacks, trying to raise potatoes and vegetables. We got into an argument with a man who used very abusive language while ordering us not to go further. Of course, he had no right to order us around. When we went on he apparently lost his senses and became crazy. He ran toward us, a heavy, long-handled army spade over his head ready to kill us, or so it seemed to me. As a weapon I carried a walking cane with a steel blade sharply pointed and able to pierce and kill a person. When this blade confronted him he knew he could not hit us without a fight and he hesitated. I had to retreat slowly to stay out of reach of his long weapon, my pregnant wife frantically pulling me away from the man. After a little while he lowered his spade and the danger was over. It all happened so fast we had no time to be afraid, but later on we realized it had been a close shave. As to law and order, times were not normal. To have been entangled in a bloody fracas, perhaps even a manslaughter case, might have meant the end of plans to go to the United States.

To make some money while waiting for our U.S. entry permit, I founded the import firm "Friedrich L. Nagel," Langenstrasse 70, Bremen, which was my father's office. We had a German friend in Cuba from whom I bought garden furniture. I cannot remember whether these transactions were profitable, but my speculations on the German stock exchange brought in substantial profits in inflated marks, which went down in real purchasing power every day. To own or try to keep paper money made no sense — it had to be exchanged into something tangible — anything from jewelry and fine paintings to grand pianos. Of course, these manipulations made inflation progress that much faster until the mark was worthless. As a gamble I left a large amount of paper marks in a German bank on deposit. At that time it represented a value of about $1,000. If the mark ever would regain its normal value of four marks to the dollar, we would have had a small fortune. But later we received a short notice from the bank in Bremen, saying the inflation had wiped out the value of our deposit and therefore the bank could not afford to keep our account on its books. We took a bad gamble, but it should be remembered that around 1920 a phenomenon called inflation was something brand new in a nation like Germany. Nobody could foresee the outcome. It was financial chaos, against which everybody fought according to their own ideas and plans.

Finally, after months of waiting, we received good news from my brother in Kentucky in August 1921. Mr. Barkley and former Secretary of State Lansing had written to the newly established U.S. passport division in Berlin to grant entry visas to my family. This consisted of myself, my wife and infant son, Fritz. My mother-in-law, being a British subject, had no trouble and went with us. Not knowing what types of quizzes we might be subjected to, we were somewhat uneasy and fearful as we entered the U.S. consul's office in Berlin. In line behind us stood an American citizen of German extraction, a Mr. Schmoller. He sensed our uneasiness and helped us a great deal in steering us over possible tricky questions asked by the examiner. If the examiner was convinced we would not make good citizens he still would refuse to visa our passports. This smiling Mr. Schmoller acted as if he knew us and things went wonderfully well. It so happened that Mr. Schmoller was fabricating pianos in Omaha, Nebraska, and because he was sailing on the same ship we became friends. On that first trip to the United States, while still on board, we bought sight unseen from Mr. Schmoller the piano that is still in my son Frank's house.

The SS. George Washington had been one of the North German Lloyd luxury liners and now was operated by an American line which had received the ship as a war reparation. Life onboard was gay and carefree. General Pershing and his staff were one of the main social attractions. When we crossed the gangplank to board this beautiful ship, we entered a new world so very different from the dismal atmosphere which had permeated everything and everybody in Germany. The rich food after years of eating anything just to stay alive was a pleasure we enjoyed tremendously, but the food and the sea made me sick. We celebrated my oldest son's second birthday on board. He had a wonderful time, going from deck chair to deck chair, visiting only the men and trying to go through their pockets. There were very few Germans in first class and the Americans we met on the ship were as friendly to us as they could be. It was a good omen.

Our train from New York reached Paducah, Kentucky, on Halloween Day in 1921. Now we could begin to build a new life. I was 29 years old and could speak only broken English. Up to now, and for some time to come, the conversation at home was in German until I became more proficient in English.

The joy we felt, and the relief to have escaped from a Germany in turmoil to this wealthy and friendly land of opportunity, has never left us.

Back home. Fritz and Dorothy pose with Nagel's parents and a niece outside the Nagel home in Bremen.

Members of the Bremen Stadtwehr, August 1919.

Freikorps troops, believed to be members of the 1st Marine Brigade von Roden, during the February 1919 Spartacus uprising in Bremen.

The Nagels, with oldest son Fritz, aboard the SS George Washington on their way to America, October 20, 1921.